FORTRAN 77

COMPUTER SCIENCE SERIES

COMPUTER SCIENCE SERIES

FORTRAN 77

Harry Katzan, Jr.
Chairman, Computer Science Department
Pratt Institute

VNR VAN NOSTRAND REINHOLD COMPANY
NEW YORK   CINCINNATI   ATLANTA   DALLAS   SAN FRANCISCO
LONDON   TORONTO   MELBOURNE

Van Nostrand Reinhold Company Regional Offices:
New York   Cincinnati   Atlanta   Dallas   San Francisco

Van Nostrand Reinhold Company International Offices:
London   Toronto   Melbourne

Library of Congress Catalog Card Number: 78-5943
ISBN: 0-442-24278-6

Manufactured in the United States of America

Published by Van Nostrand Reinhold Company
135 West 50th Street, New York, N.Y. 10020

Published simultaneously in Canada by Van Nostrand Reinhold Ltd.

15 14 13 12 11 10 9 8 7 6 5 4 3 2 1

Library of Congress Cataloging in Publication Data

Katzan, Harry
    FORTRAN 77.

    (Computer science series)
    Includes bibliographical references and index.
    1. FORTRAN (Computer program language)   I. Title.
QA76.73.F25K373   001.6'424   78-5943
ISBN 0-442-24278-6

PREFACE

The FORTRAN language was originally developed for applications that involve the manipulation of numerical data, and was released for customer use by the IBM Corporation in 1957. In the years 1957 to 1966, the language evolved as a scientific programming language and was standardized in 1966. The language has been supported by the computer industry and because of the acceptance of the FORTRAN standard of 1966, FORTRAN programs developed on one computer may be run on another computer without modification. In the short history of computers, many millions of dollars have been invested by various organizations in FORTRAN programs.

Through the years, however, FORTRAN applications have evolved from strictly numerically oriented applications to more general applications involving character and file manipulation. As a result, most computer manufacturers have extended their version of FORTRAN to include more advanced processing facilities. Clearly, the advanced features have drastically enlarged the scope of possible FORTRAN applications, but at the expense of decreased portability of FORTRAN programs. In short, a new standard was needed.

A draft of a *new* FORTRAN standard was distributed in March, 1976, and normal standardization activity has progressed since then.

The final version of the new FORTRAN standard which was recently approved is the subject of this book.

The new FORTRAN standard does not obsolete older FORTRAN programs but increases the scope of the language in the following areas: input/output facilities, data declaration facilities, subprogram facilities, construction of previously limited to integer values, and a variety of miscellaneous enhancements. More specifically, the extensions to the 1966 FORTRAN standard are listed as follows:

Input/Output Facilities

Process stream and direct access, not just sequential files

Provide list-directed, not just record oriented transmission

Provide internal (storage-to-storage) transmission

Provide statements to open and close files or inquire about file status

Provide for transmission to/from a standard system device, without having to explicitly identify the unit

Provide for additional format edit codes such as tabbing, sign control, and blank editing control

Data Declaration Facilities

Declare fixed length character strings with operators for concatenation, length, substring, assignment, and relationals

Specify symbolic constants (e.g., PARAMETER PI = 3.14159)

Save values from one invocation of a subroutine to another

Specify a main program name

Specify the implicit type rule in effect (data type determined by the first character of a name)

Define array bounds to be negative, zero, or positive integer constant expressions and from 1 to 7 dimensions

Use an array name, character substring, or implied do list in a DATA statement

Use an array name or character substring in an EQUIVA-LENCE statement

Subprogram Facilities

Specify multiple entry points to subprograms

Specify multiple returns in subroutines

Differentiate between external and intrinsic (built-in) subprograms

Specify generic names for intrinsic functions (e.g., ABS)

Specify functions of 0 arguments

Specify more than one block data subprogram

Use of Integer Expressions Rather Than Just Integers

Array subscripts

DO and implied do control parameters

Selection values for computed GO TO's

External units referred to in a BACKSPACE, ENDFILE, or REWIND statement

Miscellaneous Capabilities

DO and implied do loops that may execute 0 times and have negative incrementation parameters

Use of a format statement label in an ASSIGN statement

Use of decimal digits or a character string in a PAUSE or STOP statement

Use of a block data subprogram name in an external statement

Use of integer, real, or double precision expressions rather than just integers for DO parameters and implied DO control parameters in input/output lists

Block IF, ELSE IF, ELSE, and ENDIF statements for conditional statement execution

In addition to the extensions mentioned above, this book covers the full FORTRAN language including complete syntactical forms, examples, and semantical descriptions. Even though the book is intended to provide a definitive treatment of the new FORTRAN standard, it does so without a loss of readability or of clarity.

This book would be of particular interest to all scientists, engineers, mathematicians, and analysts that use the FORTRAN language on a regular or casual basis. Through the use of specially prepared syntactical forms, the book not only gives the specification of the new FORTRAN facilities but also the 1966 FORTRAN standard. Thus, the book serves as a handy reference as well as providing information on the new FORTRAN enhancements.

It is a pleasure to acknowledge the contributions of J. C. Noll and Wayne A. Lindo, and the valuable assistance of my wife Margaret.

CONTENTS

1 | INTRODUCTION

1.1 PURPOSE OF THE BOOK

FORTRAN is a mathematically oriented programming language, originally developed for computer applications that involve the manipulation of numerical data. (FORTRAN is an acronym for FORmula TRANslation.) FORTRAN processing facilities are available for practically all computers—either through manufacturer supplied software, through software developed "in house," or by independent software firms. The language is known and used by most engineers, scientists, mathematicians, statisticians, and business analysts on a regular or casual basis. As such, many millions of dollars have been invested by various organizations in FORTRAN programs.

1.1.1 History

The original version of FORTRAN was developed by IBM and released for customer use in 1957. The language achieved widespread acceptance and evolved as a scientific programming language in the years 1957–1966. FORTRAN was standardized in 1966 and through the use of the standard, a FORTRAN program developed for one computer system could be run on another computer system without modification.

1.1.2 Extensions

The FORTRAN language was originally developed for numerical applications and the 1966 standard reflects this class of users. Through the years, however, FORTRAN applications evolved from strictly numerically oriented applications to more general applications involving character and file manipulation. As a direct result of the situation, most computer manufacturers have enhanced their version of FORTRAN to include more advanced processing facilities. The advanced features, normally referred to as *extensions*, have enlarged the scope of potential FORTRAN applications, but at the expense of decreased portability of FORTRAN programs. In short, a new standard was needed.

1.1.3 Development of the New FORTRAN Standard

A draft version of a *new* FORTRAN standard was distributed in March, 1976, and normal standardization activity has progressed since then. A final version of the new FORTRAN standard was recently approved (September, 1977), and it is the subject of this book. The new standard is referred to as FORTRAN 77.

1.1.4 Scope of the New FORTRAN Standard

The new FORTRAN standard does not obsolete older FORTRAN programs but increases the scope of the language in the following areas: input/output facilities, data declaration facilities, subprogram facilities, constructs previously limited to integer values, and a variety of miscellaneous enhancements. A brief summary and overview of the 1977 extensions to the 1966 standard is listed as follows:

Input/Output Facilities
1. Process stream and direct access, not just sequential files
2. Provide list-directed, not just record-oriented transmission
3. Provide internal (storage-to-storage) transmission
4. Provide statements to open and close files or inquire about file status

5. Provide for transmission to/from a standard system device, without having to explicitly identify the unit
6. Provide for additional format edit codes such as tabbing, sign control, and blank editing control

Data Declaration Facilities
1. Declare fixed length character strings with operators for concatenation, length, substring, assignment, and relationals
2. Specify symbolic constants (e.g., PARAMETER PI = 3.14159)
3. Save values from one invocation of a subroutine to another
4. Specify a main program name
5. Specify the implicit type rule in effect (data type determined by the first character of a name)
6. Define array bounds to be negative, zero, or positive integer constant expressions and from 1 to 7 dimensions
7. Use an array name, character substring, or implied do list in a DATA statement
8. Use an array name or character substring in an EQUIVA-LENCE statement

Subprogram Facilities
1. Specify multiple entry points to subprograms
2. Specify multiple returns in subroutines
3. Differentiate between external and intrinsic (built-in) subprograms
4. Specify generic names for intrinsic functions (e.g., ABS)
5. Specify functions of 0 arguments
6. Specify more than one block data subprogram

Use of Integer Expressions Rather Than Just Integers
1. Array subscripts
2. DO and implied do control parameters
3. Selection values for computed GO TO's
4. External units referred to in a BACKSPACE, ENDFILE, or REWIND statement

Miscellaneous Capabilities
1. DO and implied do loops that may execute 0 times and have negative incrementation parameters
2. Use of a format statement label in an ASSIGN statement

3. Use of decimal digits or a character string in a PAUSE or STOP statement
4. Use of a block data subprogram name in an external statement
5. Use of integer, real, or double precision expressions rather than just integers for DO parameters and implied DO control parameters in input/output lists
6. Block IF, ELSE IF, ELSE, and END IF statements for conditional statement execution

The new FORTRAN standard also incorporates a variety of lexical, syntactical, and semantical improvements, as well as a more definitive specification of the processing requirements for the interpretation and execution of standard-conforming programs.

1.2 PLAN OF THE BOOK

The objective of this book is to present the technical specifications of FORTRAN 77 in as comprehensive a form as possible. The subject matter recognizes the intended audience and uses a variety of methods of presentation to cover the scope of the language. Through the use of specially prepared syntax charts, the book not only gives the specifications of FORTRAN 77 facilities but also covers the 1966 FORTRAN standard. In the latter case, the syntax charts serve as a detailed comparison of the 1966 FORTRAN standard and the new FORTRAN standard.

1.2.1 Audience

The intended audience for this book is the large class of engineers, scientists, mathematicians, statisticians and business analysts who have been exposed to FORTRAN through an academic course, an industrial seminar, or through actual experience. A reader need not be an active user of FORTRAN to benefit from the book and a casual knowledge of FORTRAN is all that is required for complete understanding. However, the book is also intended for experienced FORTRAN users who desire to know the contents of the new FORTRAN standard. Toward these ends, the book utilizes the following methods of presentation:

1. Introductory material
2. Metalanguage descriptions
3. FORTRAN 77 language examples

4. Syntax charts
5. Explanatory notes

Consequently, the reader may select the appropriate level of presentation for each of the various topics—depending upon the kind of information that is needed.

1.2.2 Scope

Collectively, the scope of the various topics and methods of presentation includes the following:

1. The correct form of statements and programs written in the FORTRAN 77 language
2. Specific rules for interpreting and executing a standard-conforming program and its data
3. The form that input data to be processed by a standard-conforming FORTRAN 77 program would take
4. The form of output data generated by a standard-conforming FORTRAN 77 program

Thus, the subject matter may be used by those persons engaged in writing compilers and interpreters for the FORTRAN 77 language, in addition to persons using the language as a programming tool.

1.2.3 Comparison

The presentation of the subject matter also provides the basis for a detailed comparison of the 1966 FORTRAN standard and the new FORTRAN standard. For example, the following syntax chart for the CALL statement:

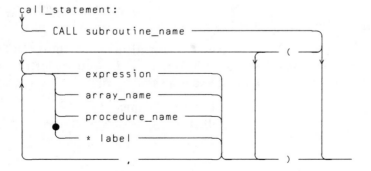

describes the syntax of the statement and indicates that the * label option for alternate returns is an extension to the 1966 standard. (More specifically, paths marked with "●" include extensions to the 1966 FORTRAN standard.) Semantic extensions to the language are discussed in the text, as are changes to the languages that realistically can not be viewed as extensions.

The various operational conventions are introduced in subsequent sections.

1.3 SYNTAX NOTATION

Two distinct syntactical conventions are used to describe the FORTRAN 77 language: Extended Backus Notation and Syntax Diagram Form. In general, the FORTRAN 77 statements and some FORTRAN 77 constructs are described in the body of the text through the use of Extended Backus Notation. Most people are familiar with Extended Backus Notation or a related set of metalanguage conventions and symbols. Syntax Diagram Form is equivalent to Extended Backus Notation or Backus-Naur Form in descriptive power and many people find it relatively easy to read. All FORTRAN 77 statements and language constructs are described in Syntax Diagram Form in either the body of the text or an appendix. An example of Syntax Diagram Form was given in the previous section.

1.3.1 Extended Backus Notation

Extended Backus Notation is a set of metalanguage conventions and symbols that is useful for describing the class of programming languages represented by FORTRAN 77. Extended Backus Notation evolved from Backus-Naur Form (BNF), which was developed for ALGOL 60. Extended Backus Notation employs eight rules and associated symbols, defined as follows:

1. A *notation variable* names a constituent of the FORTRAN language. It takes one of 3 forms: (1) Lowercase letters, possibly separated by an underscore, as in:

> function_name
> dlist
> cb

(2) A sequence of one or more lowercase letters to which a subscript has been appended, as in:

$$e_1$$
$$s_2$$

or (3) Either of the above forms that are italicized, as in:

$$nlist$$
$$d_1$$
$$typ$$
$$a$$

(In the latter case, a construct is italicized when special attention should be directed to it, as in denoting that specific entities in the description of a particular statement must be replaced when an actual statement is written.)

2. A *notation constant*, which stands for itself and is represented by capital letters, punctuation characters, or special characters. A notation constant must be written as indicated in the syntactic description. In the following statement, for example:

$$\text{ASSIGN } s \text{ TO } i$$

the keywords ASSIGN and TO are notation constants and s and i are notation variables. Similarly, in the statement:

$$\text{IF } (e) \, s_1, s_2, s_3$$

the keyword IF, the parentheses, and the commas are notation constants and the lower case subscripted letters are notation variables.

3. A set of *brackets* ([ ]) represents an option and the enclosed syntactical units can be omitted. In the following DO statement, for example,

$$\text{DO } s \, [,] \, i = e_1, e_2 [,e_3]$$

the comma following the statement number and the increment, represented by e_3, are optional and can be omitted.

4. A *syntactical unit* is a notation variable, a notation constant, or a series of notation variables or constants enclosed in brackets.

5. The *ellipses*, a series of three periods, indicates that the preced-

ing syntactic unit may be repeated one or more times in succession. In the following INTEGER statement, for example,

INTEGER $v[,v]$ . . .

the ellipses denotes that more than one variable or array, denoted by "v", may be defined with the "integer" data type. Alternately, the ellipses denotes that there is no requirement that the preceding syntactical be present at least one time.

In general, blanks may be used in FORTRAN to improve readability but have no significance, unless specifically noted.

1.3.2 Syntax Diagram Form

A syntax chart is used to give a "bird's eye view" of the structure of a programming language and has the obvious advantage of being easier to read than metalanguage notation. The "syntax diagram form" employed here is equivalent to Backus-Naur Form used with ALGOL 60 or to Extended Backus Notation.

In a syntax chart, capital letters and special characters must appear as written. Sequences of lowercase letters and the underscore characters represent syntactic units that must be replaced when a statement is written. A syntax chart takes the form of a railroad track in which switches denote the existence of syntactic alternatives. A circle "$\bigcirc$" or a half-circle "$\frown$" are used to denote how many times a path is traversed:

(n) denotes a path must be traversed exactly n times

$\frown n$ denotes a path may be traversed at most n times.

Paths in a diagram that include extensions to the 1966 FORTRAN standard are marked with a bullet, i.e., a "•", for identification. Thus, the syntax charts serve as a description of 1966 FORTRAN as well as FORTRAN 77. Examples further demonstrate the Syntax Diagram Form.

Example 1. A logical constant is described as:

logical_constant:

. TRUE .

. FALSE .

(alternatives)

This syntax chart specifies that a logical constant is either .TRUE. or .FALSE. .

Example 2. An integer constant is described as:

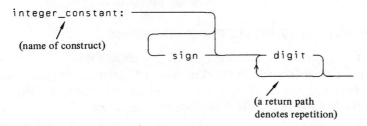

An integer constant is an optional sign followed by one or more digits.

Example 3. A statement label is described as:

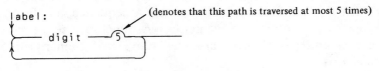

A statement label is 1 to 5 decimal digits.

Example 4. The computed goto statement is described as:

This syntax chart specifies that the concept of a goto variable in a computed goto statement has been extended to encompass an integer expression.

The advantage of the use of Syntax Diagram Form is that the charts are useful, perhaps more useful than customary metalanguage descriptions, provided that the following FORTRAN 77 characteristics are recognized:

1. The use of blank characters
2. The use of comment lines
3. The structure of initial and continuation lines

4. Context-dependent features, such as data type requirements and the uniqueness of statement labels

The syntax charts also give a clear picture of the options that are available in a FORTRAN 77 language construct.

1.4 FORTRAN 77 CONCEPTS AND TERMS

One of the most notable aspects of the FORTRAN 77 standard is the precise specification and delineation of many of the concepts and terms that are normally left undefined in other documents on the FORTRAN language. Well defined terminology helps in assuring that the FORTRAN 77 standard will be useful, regardless of the evolution of computer concepts.

1.4.1 Sequence

A *sequence* is a set of elements ordered by a one-to-one correspondence with the numbers 1, 2 through *n*. A sequence may be empty which means it contains no elements. A nonempty sequence contains a first and last element and the number of elements in a sequence is *n*.

The concept of a sequence is used in a variety of contexts in FORTRAN 77. For example, a program is a sequence of statements. Similarly, an array is a nonempty sequence of data and a character datum is a nonempty sequence of characters.

1.4.2 List

A *list* is a nonempty sequence of syntactic entities separated by commas. Examples of FORTRAN lists are:

1. Format specifiers in a FORMAT statement
2. Variable names in a DATA statement
3. Dimension declarators in an array declaration
4. Control specifications in an input or an output statement

The entities in a list are known as list items.

1.4.3 Storage Sequence and Units

The notion of a storage sequence is introduced to establish a means of referring to the manner in which data is stored without making an implicit committment to a particular form of storage technology.

A *storage sequence* is a sequence of storage units. A *storage unit* refers to the amount of storage needed to record a particular class of data. A storage unit can be a numeric storage unit or a character storage unit.

A *numeric storage unit* can be used to hold (i.e., store) an integer, real, or logical datum. Two numeric storage units in a storage sequence are needed to hold (i.e., store) a double precision or complex datum.

A *character storage unit* can be used to hold (i.e., store) one character's worth of information in a character datum. Thus, one character storage unit in a storage sequence is required for each character in a character datum. When an integer, real, logical, double precision, complex, or character datum requires more than one storage unit in a storage sequence, then the required storage units must be consecutive. No relationship is established between numeric and character storage units.

1.4.4 Association

Association refers to the identification of the same entity in a program unit or executable program by different symbolic names. Usually, association applies to data items. The form of association is determined through the process by which association is achieved and includes the following:

1. Common association through the use of common storage
2. Equivalence association through the use of the EQUIVALENCE statement
3. Argument association through the invocation of subprograms
4. Entry association within function subprograms with multiple entry points

The significance of association lies in the fact that an entity can be defined in a program segment or program unit and can subsequently be referenced by another entity of the same type.

1.4.5 Definition Status

At every point in time during the execution of a FORTRAN 77 program, each variable, array, or substring has a *definition status*, which may be either "defined" or "undefined." A defined entity has a value, which does not change until the entity is redefined with another value or becomes undefined.

An entity must be defined at the time when it is referenced, since an undefined entity has an unpredictable value. Thus, an entity must be defined prior to the time when it is referenced and must not have become undefined in the meantime. An entity is *initially defined* if it is given a value in a DATA statement, which means that the entity is in the defined state when the execution of the program is initiated. An entity may also be defined through association with an entity that has been defined.

The way in which entities can become defined or undefined is presented along with the introduction to that type of entity.

1.4.6   Reference to FORTRAN 77 Entities

The term "reference" applies to variables, arrays, substrings, and procedures. A *reference* to a variable, array, or substring is the appearance of that entity in a statement that during its execution requires the use of the value of the entity. When a reference is made to a variable, array, or substring, the value of that entity is made available but the value is not changed. The process of defining an entity—i.e., assigning it a value—is not considered to be a reference to that entity.

A reference to a procedure is the appearance of the procedure name in a statement that during its execution requires that the actions of the procedure be executed. A procedure must be available when a reference to it is made in an executable program.

1.4.7 Processor

The computer is referred to as the *processor*. However, use of the term implies slightly more than a data processing system. In the context of this book, the term "processor" refers to the computer and the means by which FORTRAN programs are translated or interpreted for execution on that computer. Thus, a processor is a computer and a FORTRAN 77 compiler or a computer and a FORTRAN 77 interpreter.

2 | FORTRAN 77 LANGUAGE CHARACTERISTICS

2.1 SCOPE OF THE CHAPTER

This chapter is a summary of the various constituents from which FORTRAN 77 programs are constructed. In general, the language characteristics of FORTRAN 77 are the same as for the 1966 FORTRAN standard and the reader who is familiar with the older standard can go directly to Chapter Three.

2.2 CHARACTER SET

The FORTRAN 77 character set consists of letters, digits, and special characters. A collating sequence is defined among the character set and special considerations apply to the use of the blank character.

2.2.1 Letters and Digits

A *letter* assumes its conventional interpretation and is one of the following 26 characters:

A B C D E F G H I J K L M N O P Q R S T U V W X Y Z

A *digit* is also defined in the conventional fashion and is one of the following 10 characters:

$$0 \quad 1 \quad 2 \quad 3 \quad 4 \quad 5 \quad 6 \quad 7 \quad 8 \quad 9$$

When a numeric value is represented, digits are interpreted to the base 10. Letters and digits are collectively referred to as *alphanumeric characters*.

2.2.2 Special Characters

The FORTRAN 77 character set includes the 13 characters listed as follows:

Character	Name of Character
(no graphic representation)	Blank
=	Equals
+	Plus
−	Minus
*	Asterisk
/	Slash
(	Left parenthesis
)	Right parenthesis
,	Comma
.	Decimal point
$	Currency symbol
'	Apostrophe
:	Colon

Other special characters may be used in FORTRAN 77 programs and as data. When used in FORTRAN 77 programs, special characters other than those defined above must be present in character literals or Hollerith constants.

The processor determines the meaning of a special character through the context in which it is used. For example, a special character may be an operator, part of a numeric constant, a character in a character literal, or may serve some other purpose in the FORTRAN 77 language.

2.2.3 Collating Sequence

The collating sequence defines the relationship between characters for purposes of ordering character strings. The ordering sequence for letters and digits is given above, with A before Z and 0 before 9. The letters and digits must not be intermixed in the collating sequence; the digits must precede the letters or the digits must follow the letters. The blank character is defined as being before the letter A and before the digit 0. No order among the special characters is defined and no specification is made as to where the special characters must be placed in the collating sequence.

2.2.4 Blank Characters

The blank character has no significance in FORTRAN 77 statements, other than in character literals and Hollerith constants, and may be used freely to improve readability. Special considerations apply to the use of the blank character in the FORTRAN 77 statement format and these considerations are presented whenever appropriate. For example, columns 1–5 of an initial FORTRAN 77 line must contain a statement label or blank characters.

2.3 IDENTIFIERS

A symbolic name is a series of characters that has special meaning to the programmer; a keyword has special meaning to the processor and is used to identify a FORTRAN 77 statement or serve as a separator. Collectively, symbolic names and keywords are classed as identifiers.

2.3.1 Symbolic Names

A *symbolic name* is a series of characters, assigned by the programmer to refer to a programmer-defined entity, such as a variable, array, program unit, or labeled common block. A symbolic name is composed of a sequence of 1–6 letters or digits, the first of which must be a letter. The syntax chart for a symbolic name is

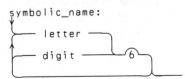

2.3.2 Keywords

A *keyword* is a sequence of characters that is significant in the FORTRAN 77 language and has meaning to the processor. A keyword is used to identify a FORTRAN 77 statement or serve as a separator in a FORTRAN 77 statement. Some typical statement identifiers are REAL, FORMAT, and READ. Two separators are TO and THEN.

There are no reserved words in FORTRAN 77 so that a symbolic name may assume the exact sequence of characters as a keyword. The processor determines the meaning of a sequence of characters by the context in which the characters are used.

2.4 STATEMENT STRUCTURE

A FORTRAN 77 program unit, such as a main program or subprogram, consists of a sequence of lines that are ordered by the succession in which they are presented to the processor. A *line* consists of 72 character positions that are numbered consecutively from 1 to 72, going left to right, and called *columns*. Lines are classified as comment lines, initial lines, or continuation lines.

2.4.1 Comment Lines

A comment line is determined as follows:

1. There is a C in column 1.
2. There is an asterisk in column 1.
3. The line is completely blank. If the input medium consists of a sequence of more than 72 columns, such as an 80 column or 96 column punched card, then columns 1 through 72 are blank for this type of comment line.

Comment lines specified with either a C or an asterisk in column 1 may have any sequence of characters in columns 2 through 72.

A comment line may be placed anywhere in a program unit and does not affect the executable program in any way. One or more comment lines may be placed before the first line of a program unit, between two FORTRAN 77 statements, between an initial statement line and its first continuation line, or between two continuation lines.

2.4.2 Initial Line

The first and possibly the only line of a FORTRAN 77 statement is termed the *initial line*. Columns one through five of an initial line must be blank or contain a statement label, i.e., a statement number. Column 6 must be blank or contain the digit 0. The FORTRAN 77 statement or a portion of a FORTRAN 77 statement is placed in columns 7 through 72. The remaining columns, if any, of an initial line may be blank or be used for identification and a statement sequence number.

2.4.3 Continuation Lines

A *continuation line* contains a continuation of a FORTRAN 77 statement and has the following characteristics:

1. Columns 1 through 5 must be blank.
2. Column 6 must contain a nonblank or a nonzero character. Column 6 is frequently used to number the continuation lines.

As with the initial line, columns 7 through 72 of a continuation line are used to represent portions of a FORTRAN 77 statement and the remaining columns may be blank or be used for identification and a statement sequence number.

2.4.4 Blank Lines

A line that is blank in columns 1 through 72 is a comment line, as specified above. The FORTRAN 77 standard does not specifically cover an initial line with a statement label and continuation lines that contain only blank characters in columns 7 through 72. By default, lines in the two latter categories satisfy the definition of initial and continuation lines, respectively, and a reasonable interpretation would be that they are valid instances of the respective type of line.

2.4.5 FORTRAN 77 Statements

A FORTRAN 77 statement is entered to the processor in columns 7 through 72 of an initial line and as many as 19 continuation lines. Thus, a FORTRAN 77 statement may occupy 1320, i.e., 20 X 66, characters. However, the blank characters in FORTRAN 77 statements that are ignored by the processor are counted in the maximum of 1320 characters.

All FORTRAN 77 statements must begin with a new initial line, except when part of the logical IF statement which incorporates certain FORTRAN 77 statements as part of its normal statement structure.

The END statement denotes the end of a FORTRAN 77 program unit and no other statement may have an initial line that contains END as its first three nonblank characters.

2.4.6 Statement Numbers

A *statement number*, which is referred to in the FORTRAN 77 standard document as a "statement label," is a means of labeling a FORTRAN 77 statement so that it can be referred to in another FORTRAN 77 statement. A statement number is placed in columns 1 through 5 of an initial line and consists of 1–5 digits—one of which must be nonzero. The syntax chart for a statement number is given as follows:

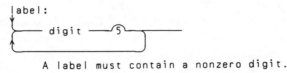

A label must contain a nonzero digit.

The number may be placed anywhere in columns 1 through 5. Leading blanks and zeros are not significant in establishing the value of a statement number.

The scope of a statement number is the program unit in which it is included and the same value may not be used to number more than one FORTRAN 77 statement. *It is not necessary to number a FORTRAN 77 statement.* However, only statements that have been numbered may be referred to in other FORTRAN 77 statements. A FORTRAN 77 statement may be numbered, even if it is not referred to and any or all statements may be numbered.

2.4.7 Form of a FORTRAN 77 Statement

All FORTRAN 77 statements with the exception of the assignment and statement function statements begin with a keyword. The keyword is used by the processor to identify the type of statement. Some examples follow:

Statement	*Comment*
REAL APPLE(50),BLIST(3,75)	Keyword is REAL
GOTO 400	Keyword is GOTO

IF (R**2-X .LT. EPS) RETURN   Keywords are IF and
                                 RETURN

R=.5*(X/R+R)   No keyword; this is an
                                 assignment statement.

The statement function, covered later, defines an internal function subprogram and takes a similar form to the assignment statement.

2.5 PROGRAM ORGANIZATION

In FORTRAN 77, statements are grouped to form program units and an executable program is comprised of one or more program units. As with many of the other sections in this book, some knowledge of the FORTRAN language is needed for full comprehension of the subject matter. However, it is possible for the reader to review this material after the reading of other parts of the book has been completed.

2.5.1 Program Unit

A *program unit* is defined as either a main program or a subprogram. The program unit determines the scope for symbolic names and statement numbers so that unless explicit measures are taken, an entity defined implicitly or explicitly in one program unit is not known by the processor when processing another program unit.

A program unit consists of a sequence of FORTRAN 77 statements and optional comment lines. A program unit always has an END statement as its final statement.

2.5.2 Main Program

The *main program* is the program unit that receives control when an executable program is placed in execution by the processor. A main program is a program unit that is identified by having a PROGRAM statement as its first statement or by the fact that it does not have a FUNCTION, SUBROUTINE, or BLOCK DATA statement as its first statement.

2.5.3 Subprograms

A *subprogram* is a program unit that receives execution control of the processor by being referenced or called in an appropriate manner by a FORTRAN 77 statement in a main program or another sub-program. A subprogram is identified by having a FUNCTION or SUBROUTINE statement as its first statement. The FUNCTION and SUBROUTINE statements specify function and subroutine subprograms, respectively.

2.5.4 Procedures

A program segment that performs an operational function in a general sense is known as a *procedure*. Three kinds of procedures are recognized in FORTRAN 77: external procedures, statement functions, and intrinsic functions. An *external procedure* is a function or a subroutine subprogram and the word "external" denotes that the program unit is processed (i.e., compiled or interpreted) independently of the referencing or calling program unit. A *statement function* is a single statement that defines a function that is processed along with the program unit in which it is included. An *intrinsic function* is an operational function, such as the square root or trigonometric sine, that is defined as part of the FORTRAN 77 programming language.

An external procedure may also exist as a non-FORTRAN sub-program. This definition permits the capability to be established of allowing subprograms written in assembler language or another higher level language to be referenced or called by a FORTRAN 77 program unit.

2.5.5 BLOCK DATA Program Unit

A program unit in which the first statement is a BLOCK DATA statement is commonly known as a "block data subprogram." A BLOCK DATA program unit may not contain executable statements and is used to initialize common storage.

2.5.6 Executable Program

An *executable program* consists of one main program and zero or more external procedures and block data program units. An executable program may not consist of more than one main program, but may contain one or more of *each* of the following entities:

1. Function subprogram

2. Subroutine subprogram
3. Block data program unit
4. Non-FORTRAN coded external procedure

The main program of an executable program may not contain ENTRY or RETURN statements, and execution of a program is terminated when a STOP statement is executed in any program unit or the END statement is executed in the main program.

The execution time characteristics of FORTRAN 77 are covered in a later section.

2.5.7 Order of Statements in a Program Unit

Table 2.1 gives the order that statements may be placed in a program unit. Vertical boundaries in the table denote statements that can be interspersed. Horizontal boundaries denote classes of statements that cannot be interspersed. For example:

1. Comment lines can be interspersed with any kind of statement, but must precede the END statement.
2. The PROGRAM, FUNCTION, SUBROUTINE, or BLOCK DATA statement must be the first statement in a program unit.
3. PARAMETER statements may be interspersed with IMPLICIT and other specification statements, but must precede DATA statements.
4. Statement function statements must precede all executable statements.

Table 2.1 is supplemented by the following rules:

1. A FORMAT statement may be placed anywhere within a program unit.
2. An ENTRY statement may be placed anywhere within a program unit, except in the range of a DO loop or between a block IF statement and its corresponding END IF statement.
3. All specification statements (i.e., the IMPLICIT statement and other specification statements) must be placed before all DATA statements, statement function statements, and executable statements.
4. All statement function statements must precede the first executable statement.

TABLE 2.1   REQUIRED ORDER OF STATEMENTS AND COMMENT
            LINES IN FORTRAN 77

	PROGRAM, FUNCTION, SUBROUTINE, or BLOCK DATA Statement		
Comment Lines	FORMAT and ENTRY Statements	PARAMETER Statements	IMPLICIT Statements
			Other Specification Statements
		DATA Statements	Statement Function Statements
			Executable Statements
	END Statement		

5. DATA statements may be placed anywhere as long as they follow PARAMETER, IMPLICIT, and other specification statements.

6. The IMPLICIT statements must precede other specification statements, with the exception of PARAMETER statements.

7. A specification statement (i.e., the IMPLICIT statement and other specification statements) that specifies the type of the symbolic name that is to be used as an identifier for a constant value must precede the PARAMETER statement that associates the symbolic name with the particular constant.

8. The PARAMETER statement associating a symbolic name with a constant value must precede all statements that contain (i.e., use) the symbolic name.

Some obvious observations can also be made. A comment line may precede a PROGRAM, FUNCTION, SUBROUTINE, or BLOCK DATA statement but may not follow the END statement. A DATA statement may appear anywhere after the specification statements since its values are assigned prior to execution of a program unit.

The above rules only apply to program units that permit or include the specific statements involved.

3 | DATA TYPES AND CONSTANT VALUES

3.1 DATA TYPES

Six types of data are explicitly permitted in FORTRAN 77:

> Integer
> Real
> Double precision
> Complex
> Logical
> Character

In addition, Hollerith data may be specified in FORMAT statements.

In general, three kinds of entities have a data type: constants, data names, and procedures. The data type of a constant is determined by the manner in which it is written.

The data type of a data name is determined explicitly through a type statement or implicitly in one of the following ways:

1. By the first character in its identifier. A first letter of I, J, K, L, M, or N implies an integer data type. Any other letter implies a real data type.

2. Through an IMPLICIT statement that changes the default implied data type.

An implicit declaration of a data type only applies in the absence of an explicit data type declaration. A data name is used to identify a variable, an array, or a parameter. A parameter is a constant that is assigned a symbolic name through the use of a PARAMETER statement.

Three kinds of procedures can have a data type: the external function, the statement function, and the intrinsic function. The data type of an external function and a statement function determines the data type of the data item returned when the function is referenced in an expression. The data type of an external or statement function is determined by its name, which may be declared explicitly in a type statement or implicitly by the first letter of the name in the absence of an explicit data type declaration. As with data names, function names beginning with I, J, K, L, M, or N are implicitly declared to be of type integer. Any other letter implies a real type. The IMPLICIT statement may be used to change the default implied data type. An explicit declaration of the type of an external function may also be specified in the FUNCTION statement, and an IMPLICIT statement within an external function can affect the data type of the function in which it is included.

Intrinsic functions are identified by generic function names that do not require an explicit or implicit type declaration. The data type of an intrinsic function is determined by the data type of its argument. The FORTRAN 77 processor supplies the reference to an appropriate processing routine. Although the data type of an intrinsic function need not be declared, an explicit data type declaration is permitted.

In general, a data type is applicable to values that can be used in a FORTRAN 77 expression—hence the categories of constants, data names, and functions covered above. For this reason, a data type for symbolic names that identify main programs, subroutines, common blocks, and block data program units is not meaningful, and therefore, is not assigned. A FORTRAN 77 statement number is a unique positive integer constant, but a data type has no meaning in this context either.

3.2 CONSTANTS AND VALUES

A *constant* is a data value that does not change during the execution of a program. In FORTRAN 77, the data type of a constant may be arithmetic, logical, or character. A *value* is a data item associated with a variable, array element, function reference, or expression that can occur during the execution of a FORTRAN 77 program. For example, a variable may be defined or undefined. The value of a defined variable is the data item assigned to it in an assignment or an input statement.

The manner in which a constant is written (i.e., its form) specifies its value and its data type. With the PARAMETER statement, a constant may be assigned a symbolic name. However, the symbolic name of one constant may not be used to form another constant. Except in a character constant, which is enclosed in quote marks, a blank character occurring within a constant has no effect upon its value and is ignored by the processor.

Four types of arithmetic constants are permitted: integer, real, double precision, and complex. An arithmetic constant may be signed or unsigned. A signed constant has a leading plus or minus sign, which denotes a positive or negative value, respectively. An unsigned constant does not have a leading plus or minus sign and a positive value is specified. An optionally signed arithmetic constant may be signed or unsigned, as appropriate to that type of constant. Integer, real, and double precision constants may be optionally signed.

The syntax chart for FORTRAN 77 constants is given in Figure 3.1.

3.3 INTEGER DATA

An integer data item is an exact representation of an integral number. In FORTRAN 77, an entity with an integer data type may exist as a constant, a parameter, an integer variable, an element in an integer array, a value of a function reference, or the value of an expression. An integer data item occupies one numeric storage unit in a storage sequence and may assume a positive, negative, or zero value.

An *integer constant* may specify a positive, negative, or zero value and is always written as an optional sign followed by a string of

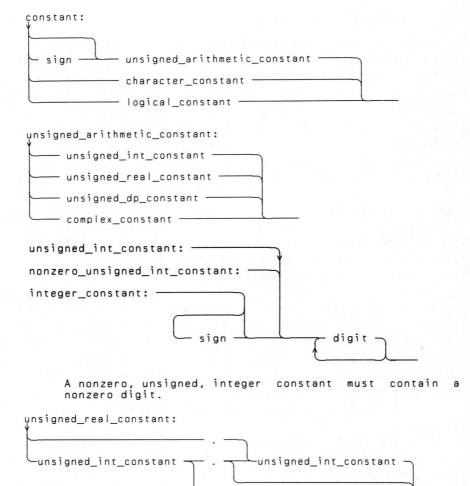

A nonzero, unsigned, integer constant must contain a nonzero digit.

Figure 3.1 Syntax chart for FORTRAN 77 constants.

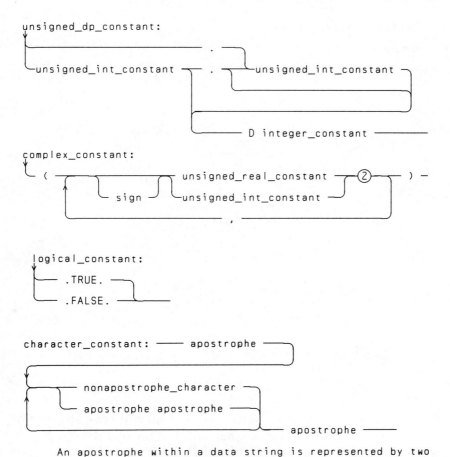

unsigned_dp_constant:

complex_constant:

logical_constant:

character_constant:

An apostrophe within a data string is represented by two consecutive apostrophes with no intervening blanks.

Figure 3.1 Syntax chart for FORTRAN 77 constants (continued).

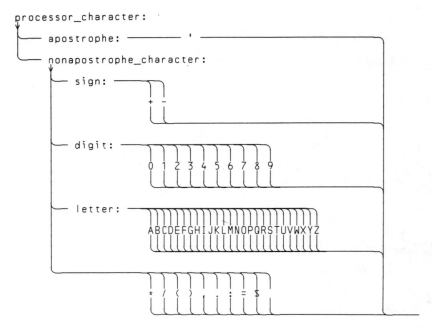

A blank is a processor character. The set of processor characters may include additional characters recognized by the processor.

Figure 3.1 Syntax chart for FORTRAN 77 constants (continued).

decimal digits that are interpreted as a decimal number. The form of an integer constant is given in the syntax chart of Figure 3.1. The following examples demonstrate valud and invalid cases of integer constants:

Valid Integer Constants	Invalid Integer Constants	
0	54.	(contains a decimal point)
75	3,216,193	(contains imbedded commas)
+230	-2.236	(contains a decimal point and
-9342605		fraction)

The maximum magnitude of an integer data item is determined by the size of the numeric storage unit.

3.4 REAL DATA

A real data item is an approximation to a real number and is dependent upon the processor's representation of this type of data.* In FORTRAN 77, an entity with a real data type may exist as a constant, a parameter, a real variable, an element in a real array, a value of a function reference, or the value of an expression. A real data item occupies one numeric storage unit in a storage sequence and may assume a positive, negative, or zero value.

A *real constant* may specify a positive, negative, or zero value and is written as one of the following three forms:

1. A basic real constant
2. A basic real constant followed by a real exponent
3. An integer constant followed by a real exponent

A basic real constant is an optional sign followed by a string of decimal digits with a decimal point. An integer constant was defined previously. A real exponent is the letter E followed by a signed or unsigned one or two digit integer constant, denoting a base 10 multiplier.

The value of the real constant is then either the basic real constant, or in the case of the real exponent, it is the basic real or integer constant multiplied by the power of 10 following the letter E in the exponent. A real constant is interpreted as a decimal number.

The form of a real constant is given in the syntax chart of Figure 3.1. The following examples demonstrate valid and invalid cases of real constants:

Valid Real Constants	*Numeric Value*
-1.5	-1.5
3E5	+300000 (which is equivalent to 3×10^5)
+.123E-3	+.000123

---

*Usually, real data items are represented as floating-point numbers, analogous to scientific representation, wherein a real value is comprised of an algebraic sign, a fraction, and an exponent. For example, –51.234 might be represented in decimal as $-.51234 \times 10^2$. The fraction of a floating point number gives its precision and the exponent of the number gives its range. The fact that a real data item is an approximation to a real number is caused by the methods used for floating point arithmetic and the base (i.e., binary, decimal, etc.) used to store the exponent and fraction.

Valid Real Constants	*Numeric Value*
−7.45E−14	−7.45×10^{-14}
5.	+5
−6389.1E21	−6389.1×10^{21}
1.23E0	+1.23 (which is equivalent to 1.23×10^{0})

Invalid Real Constants	*Reason*
5	Missing a decimal point or exponent
1,234.5	Contains a comma
.123−3	Missing the exponent designator E
−6.1E	Missing a one or two digit constant following the E
1.23456D50	Incorrect exponent designator for a *real* constant. (This is, however, a valid double precision constant)

The maximum magnitude and precision of a real constant is determined by the size of the numeric storage unit and the method of representation. The integer portion of a real constant may contain more digits than the precision used by the processor to approximate the value of the corresponding real number.

3.5 DOUBLE PRECISION DATA

A double precision data item is an approximation to a real number and is dependent upon the processor's representation of data—as in real data. The difference between real and double precision data is that with double precision data, more digits of precision are maintained than with real data.

In FORTRAN 77, an entity with a double precision data type may exist as a constant, a parameter, a double precision variable, an element in a double precision array, a value of a function reference, or the value of an expression. A double precision data item occupies two numeric storage units in a storage sequence and may assume a positive, negative, or zero value.

A *double precision constant* may specify a positive, negative, or zero value and is written as one of the following forms:

1. A basic real constant followed by a double precision exponent
2. An integer constant followed by a double precision exponent

Basic real and integer constants were defined previously. A double precision exponent is the letter D followed by a signed or unsigned one or two digit integer constant, denoting a base 10 multiplier.

The value of the double precision constant is then either the basic real or integer constant multiplied by the power of 10 following the letter D in the exponent. A double precision constant is interpreted as a decimal number.

The form of a real constant is given in the syntax chart of Figure 3.1. The following examples demonstrate valid and invalid forms of double precision constants:

Valid Double Precision Constants	*Numeric Value*
1D2	+100
.123456789101112D0	+.123456789101112
6.89D-8	+6.89$\times 10^{-8}$
-4.D+16	-4$\times 10^{16}$

Invalid Double Precision Constants	*Reason*
-1.2345678910	Missing D exponent designator
.123456789101112E0	Incorrect exponent designator
.123,456,789D5	Embedded commas
.123'456'789D5	Embedded apostrophes
7.8912D	Missing a one or two digit constant following the D

The maximum magnitude and precision of a double precision constant is determined by the size of the numberic storage units, used for storage of the double precision value, and the method of representation. The integer portion of a double precision constant may contain more digits than the precision used by the processor to approximate the value of the corresponding real number.

3.6 COMPLEX DATA

A complex data item is an approximation to a complex number and is dependent upon the processor's representation of real data. In FORTRAN 77, an entity with a complex data type may exist as a constant, a parameter, a complex variable, an element in a complex array, a value of a function reference, or the value of an expression. A complex data item occupies two consecutive numeric storage units in a storage sequence, representing a pair of values of real data type. The first component of the pair represents the real part of the complex data item and the second component of the pair represents the imaginary part of the complex data item. The real and imaginary components of a complex data item may assume positive, negative, or zero values.

A *complex constant* is a pair of either real or integer constants, separated by a comma, and enclosed in parentheses. The first constant in the pair is the real part; the second constant in the pair is imaginary. Either or both of the real or integer constants in the complex constant may be positive, negative, or zero. The form of a complex constant is given in the syntax chart of Figure 3.1. The following examples demonstrate valid and invalid cases of complex constants:

Valid Complex Constants	*Numeric Value*
(4.61, -6.81)	4.61 - 6.81i
(-10,5)	-10+5i
(.4E2,-.31E-1)	40 - .031i

Invalid Complex Constants	*Reason*
(9, 1.23)	Combination of integer and real constants
(2E3, 4D5)	Double precision constant

A complex constant is always stored as a pair of real values, and the maximum magnitude and precision of the real constants are determined by the conditions established for real data. The real or integer components of a complex constant must adhere to the conventions given previously for writing real or integer constants.

3.7 LOGICAL DATA

A logical data item may be used to denote a "true" or a "false" value. In FORTRAN 77, an entity with a logical data type may exist as a constant, a parameter, a logical variable, an element in a logical array, a value of a function reference, or the value of an expression. A logical data item occupies one numeric storage unit in a storage sequence.

A *logical constant* may specify a true or false value as follows:

Logical Constant	Logical Value
.TRUE.	True
.FALSE.	False

The words TRUE and FALSE must be preceded and followed by periods. The form of a logical constant is given in the syntax chart of Figure 3.1.

3.8 CHARACTER DATA

A character data item is a string of one or more characters. In FORTRAN 77, an entity with a character data type may exist as a constant, a parameter, a character variable, an element in a character array, a value of a function reference, or the value of an expression. Each character in a character data item occupies one character storage unit in a storage sequence, and successive characters in a character data item occupy correspondingly successive character storage units in a storage sequence.

The characters that comprise a character data item are numbered consecutively from 1 going from left to right and any character in the processor's character set may be represented—including the blank character and the apostrophe, which is also used as a delimiter. The length of a character data item is the number of characters in the character constant or in the storage sequence used to store the character data item.

A *character constant* is a string of characters enclosed in apostrophe characters. The apostrophes, used as delimiters, are not part of the character constant but all intervening characters are part of the character constant. Within a character constant, an apostrophe is represented by two successive apostrophes without an intervening blank character. The form of a character constant is given in the syntax chart of Figure 3.1. The following examples demonstrate valid and invalid character constants:

Valid Character Constants	Length	Value
'TEA FOR TWO'	11	T E A F O R T W O

Valid Character Constants	Length	Value
'DON''T'	5	`D O N ' T`
'54 RIGHT+/'	10	`5 4   R I G H T + /`

Invalid Character Constants	Reason
5HTITLE	Not enclosed in apostrophes
"TEA FOR TWO"	Not enclosed in apostrophes
'ALL RIGHT	Terminating apostrophe missing
' '	Length of character constant cannot be zero

The length of a character constant must be greater than zero.

3.9 HOLLERITH DATA

The Hollerith data type is defined in FORTRAN 77 for compatability with existing systems. However, the extent of the Hollerith data type is limited to Hollerith constants and a specific delineation of cases in which they can be used.

A *Hollerith constant* is a string of characters that takes the form:

$$n\text{H}\underbrace{xxx\ldots x}_{n \text{ characters}}$$

where n is a nonzero unsigned integer constant and the x's represent characters in the processor's character set. The length of the Hollerith constant is n and the constant is composed of the n characters that follow the H in sequence. The following examples demonstrate valid forms of Hollerith constants:

Valid Hollerith Constants	Length	Value
11HTEA FOR TWO	11	`T E A   F O R   T W O`
5HDON'T	5	`D O N ' T`
10HALL, RIGHT	10	`A L L ,   R I G H T`

The length of a Hollerith constant is always n—the unsigned nonzero integer constant that precedes the H. In a FORTRAN 77 program, a Hollerith constant may only appear in a DATA statement, in the argument list of a CALL statement, or in a FORMAT statement.

A Hollerith constant may be stored as an integer, real, or a logical variable. When a variable is assigned a Hollerith value, it becomes undefined for use as an arithmetic or logical variable. Hollerith data may be assigned to a variable through the DATA statement, as in:

```
        INTEGER ANAME
        DATA ANAME/4HJOHN/
```

or in a READ statement, as in:

```
        LOGICAL BIG
        READ(5,9000)BIG
9000    FORMAT(A4)
```

The manner in which Hollerith data is assigned to FORTRAN 77 variables is dependent upon the number of characters that can be stored in one numeric storage unit; let that value be *len*. Let the number of characters in a Hollerith data item be n. If $n > len$, then the rightmost *len* characters of the Hollerith data item are stored. If $n < len$, then the Hollerith data item is stored and extended on the right with *len-n* blank characters.

The uses of Hollerith data as a format specification or as an argument in a CALL statement are covered with the respective facilities. The use of Hollerith data with the A edit descriptor in a FORMAT statement is covered with the other edit descriptors.

4 | DATA STRUCTURES

4.1 VARIABLES

A variable is an entity with the following properties:

1. A variable name
2. A type
3. A value

The variable name must adhere to the rules given previously for a symbolic name and is established as a variable name through a type statement or through the process of definition in a FORTRAN 77 program. The type of a variable is established implicitly or explicitly, as covered previously. A variable may not be referenced unless it has been defined through an input statement, an assignment statement, or through association with a variable or element of an array that has been defined.

4.2 CHARACTER SUBSTRINGS

A character substring is a set of contiguous characters that exist as a part of a character data item. A substring must not be empty and has a character data type, so that it may be used in a character expression. A substring is specified through a substring name, and through the use of the substring name, the corresponding substring may be defined or referenced.

4.2.1 Substring Name

A substring is specified with a substring name that takes one of the following forms:

$$v([e_1]:[e_2])$$
$$a(s[,s]\ldots)([e_1]:[e_2])$$

where:

   v is a character variable name
   a is a character array name
   e_1 and e_2 are integer expressions, referred to as substring
       expressions
   s is a subscript

The expression e_1 denotes the leftmost character position of the substring relative to the beginning of the "parent" character data item* while e_2 is the rightmost character position. Thus, C(I:J) denotes the Ith through Jth characters of character variable C and D(3,2) (I:J) denotes the Ith through Jth characters of the character data item located in the 3rd row and 2nd column of character array D. More specifically, if:

   CHARACTER ABT*8, BLDG (10,5)*12
   ABT = 'VARIABLE'
   BLDG(2,4) = 'WINE FOR ONE'

then the substring name ABT(5:8) has a character value of "ABLE" and the substring name BLDG(2,4)(6:8) has a character value of "FOR". (In the CHARACTER type statement, character variable ABT is declared as having a string length of 8 and each element of character array BLDG has a string length of 12.)

The length of a character substring is e_2-e_1+1.

---

*Remember that the character positions in a string are numbered consecutively from left to right starting with 1.

4.2.2 Substring Expression

The expressions e_1 and e_2 in a substring name are referred to as substring expressions.   If *len* is the length of the "parent" character data item, then the following relationship must hold:

$$1 \leqslant e_1 \leqslant e_2 \leqslant len$$

when e_1 and e_2 are evaluated at the point of reference.

In the definition of this substring name, it should be noted that the parentheses enclosing e_1 and e_2 and the separating colon must not be omitted. If e_1 is omitted, a default value of 1 is used by the processor.   Similarly, if e_2 is omitted, then a value of *len* is used by the processor. If both e_1 and e_2 are omitted, then $v(:)$ is equivalent to v and $a(s[,s]\ldots)$ $(:)$ is equivalent to $a(s[,s]\ldots)$.

A substring expression may be any valid integer expression, provided that a function reference in one substring expression does not affect the value of the other substring expression in the same substring name.

4.3 ARRAYS

An array is a set of data items of the same type that occupies consecutive storage units in a storage sequence.   Each array has the following properties:

1. An array name
2. A data type
3. A set of data values termed array elements
4. A number denoting the number of dimensions
5. An extent for each dimension
6. A lower and upper array bounds for each dimension

An array can be specified by array name alone when reference or definition is made to the array as a whole, or an element in the array may be specified by the array name followed by an appropriate subscript. In an array, each element may be defined or undefined.

4.3.1 Array Name and Type

An array name adheres to the rules given previously for a symbolic name and is established through a dimension, common, or a type statement. All arrays must be declared in FORTRAN 77 and can be of any of the data types mentioned previously—i.e., integer, real, double precision, complex, logical, or character. The data type of an array is declared explicitly in a type statement or implicitly through the first character in the array name. An array can have from one to seven dimensions.

4.3.2 Storage of an Array

Storage for an array is allocated in the program unit in which it is declared, except in subprograms in which the array name is specified as a parameter to be subsequently passed as an argument. The declaration of an array in a program unit in which storage for the array is actually allocated is termed an *actual array declaration*. The declaration of an array in a subprogram in which the array name is passed as a parameter is termed a *dummy array declaration.* In an actual array declaration, the number of dimensions of an array and the size of each dimension must not be variable. In a dummy array declaration, the dimensions of an array may be adjustable or have an assumed size. The topic of array declaration is covered in more detail in later chapters.

Arrays in FORTRAN 77 are stored in what is known as "column order," which means that the leftmost subscript varies first, as compared to row (or lexicographic) order in which the rightmost subscript varies first.

4.3.3 Dimensions of an Array

The specification of an array is made with a DIMENSION, COMMON, or type statement, such as the following:

REAL array-declarator [,array-declarator]. . .

where the "array declarator" has the general form:

$$a(d[,d]. . .)$$

in which a is the symbolic name of the array and d is a dimension specification of the form:

$$[d_1:]\, d_2$$

d_1 is the lower subscript bound and d_2 is the upper subscript bound. If d_1 is omitted, it is assumed to be one. Thus, an array specification such as:

$$REAL\ A(2,0:3),B(-1:6)$$

would contain the following elements:

Array A	*Array B*
A(1,0)	B(-1)
A(2,0)	B(0)
A(1,1)	B(1)
A(2,1)	B(2)
A(1,2)	B(3)
A(2,2)	B(4)
A(1,3)	B(5)
A(2,3)	B(6)

The size of each dimension is known as its *extent*. In the above example, A has a row extent of 2 and column extent of 4. B has an extent of 8.

4.3.4 Array Subscript

A distinct element of an array is defined or referenced through the use of a subscript, which has the following form:

$$(s[,s]\ldots)$$

where s is a subscript expression. Each subscript expression serves as an index to its respective dimension and must lie within the subscript bounds for that dimension. The subscript expressions necessary to select an element of an array are separated by commas and enclosed in parentheses. Collectively, the term *subscript* refers to the parentheses, the subscript expressions, and the commas.

A *subscript expression* must be a valid integer expression and must contain no function references that affect other subscript expressions in the same subscript.

4.3.5 Selection of an Element of an Array

An element of an array is selected through an *array element name*, that takes the form:

$$a(s[,s]\ldots)$$

where *a* is the array name and the *s*'s are subscript expressions. The number of subscript expressions must be equal to the number of dimensions specified in the array declarator for the named array. Using the following specification, for example:

$$\text{REAL } A(2,0:3), B(-1:6)$$

A(2,1) denotes the element located in row 2 and column 1 of array A. This is the fourth element in the storage sequence occupied by array A. Similarly, B(1) denotes the element selected through a subscript expression with a value of 1, which is the third element in the storage sequence occupied by array B.

Elements in an array are selected through a subscript value which is calculated at the point of reference using the array dimensions and the corresponding subscript expressions. This is a storage management topic, covered in a later chapter.

5 | EXPRESSIONS

5.1 OVERVIEW

An expression is a sequence of operands, operators, and parentheses that specify an arithmetic, a character, a relational, or a logical computation. The evaluation of an expression is always a value that is used in the execution of the FORTRAN 77 statement that contains the expression. The use of expressions has been generalized in FORTRAN standard so that expressions may be used in instances previously limited to variables or elements of an array. Mixed-mode expressions and generalized subscripts are also permitted in the new FORTRAN. The syntax diagram form for expressions in FORTRAN 77 is lengthy and is contained in the appendix.

5.2 ARITHMETIC EXPRESSIONS

An arithmetic expression represents a numeric value obtained through a numeric computation or as the value of an arithmetic constant, an arithmetic parameter, an arithmetic variable, or an element of an arithmetic array. Accordingly, the simplest form of an arithmetic expression is an arithmetic constant, an arithmetic parameter, an arithmetic variable reference, an arithmetic array reference, or an arithmetic function reference.* Through the use of arithmetic operators and parenthesis, sophisticated sequences of calculations can be specified.

5.2.1 Arithmetic Operators

Five arithmetic operators are defined in FORTRAN 77:

Operator	Name
**	Exponentiation
/	Division
*	Multiplication
–	Subtraction or Negation
+	Addition or Identity

The operators + and – can be used with either one or two operands; *, /, and ** can be used only with two operands.

The form and meaning of the five arithmetic operators are given in Table 5.1. The interpretation of an arithmetic expression is based on a precedence relation among the arithmetic operators, which is listed as follows:

Operator	Priority
**	highest
* and /	↓
+ and –	lowest

The precedence rules apply to sequential operators in an expression such that operators with a higher priority are executed before operators with a lower priority. Thus, in the expression:

$$A+B**C*D$$

The operators are effectively executed in the following order:

1. B**C   Denote the result by X yielding   A+X*D
2. X*D   Denote the result by Y yielding   A+Y
3. A+Y   Giving the final result.

Similarly, evaluation of the expression $-R**2$ when R is equal to 3 yields a result of -9, since the negation operator is executed last.

*An arithmetic function reference may in fact require numeric computations in the evaluation of its arguments and may specify numeric computations in the body of the function.

TABLE 5.1   FORM AND MEANING OF ARITHMETIC OPERATORS*

Form	Meaning
$x_1 ** x_2$	Exponentiation: x_1 raised to the x_2 power
x_1 / x_2	Division: x_1 divided by x_2
$x_1 * x_2$	Multiplication: x_1 multiplied by x_2
$x_1 - x_2$	Subtraction: x_1 minus x_2
$x_1 + x_2$	Addition: x_1 plus x_2
$-x_2$	Negation: 0 minus x_2
$+x_2$	Identity: 0 plus x_2

*(x_1 and x_2 denote arithmetic operands.)

5.2.2 Arithmetic Operands

Arithmetic operands must specify values that have a data type of integer, real, double precision, or complex. Moreover, certain rules apply to the manner in which specific operands may be combined in an arithmetic expression. This subject is covered later. The value used as an operand may be obtained from an arithmetic constant, an arithmetic parameter, an arithmetic variable, an arithmetic array reference, an arithmetic function reference, or from the value of a sequence of operations previously executed in the evaluation of the arithmetic expression. Since each of the ways of obtaining an arithmetic value constitutes an arithmetic expression, then it can be said that the operands to an arithmetic operator must be arithmetic expressions.

5.2.3 Structure of Arithmetic Expressions

One means of defining exactly that which constitutes an arithmetic expression is to use a hierarchy of definitions, starting with that of an arithmetic expression. The operands covered in the previous section exist at the lowest level in the hierarchy. This hierarchical method of exposition is suggested by Figure 5.1, which contains a pictorial representation of the form of an arithmetic expression.

The *arithmetic expression* exists at the highest level in the hierarchy and its forms are:

> Term
> + term
> - term
> Arithmetic expression + term
> Arithmetic expression - term

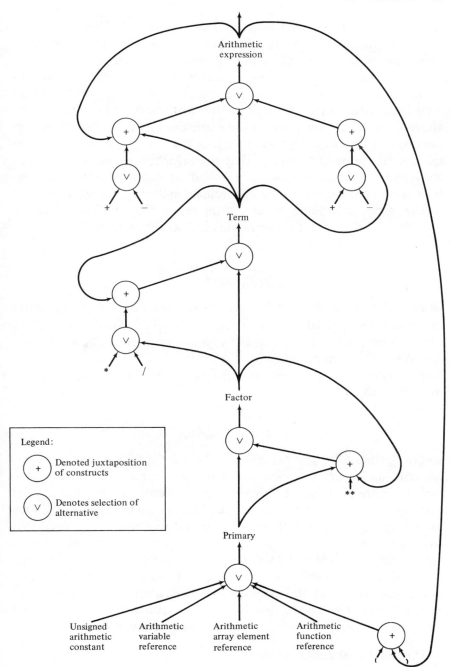

Figure 5.1   Pictorial representation of the form of an arithmetic expression.

where "term" is defined below. This definition effectively states that an arithmetic expression may begin with a leading plus or minus sign, that additive operators in sequence are executed from left to right, and that two arithmetic operators may not appear in succession. Thus, for example, in the expression A∗B−C, the subexpression A∗B is executed first because it is the "arithmetic expression" in the above definition. Similarly, in the expression A+B∗C, the subexpression B∗C is executed first because it is the "term" in the above definition. It follows, therefore, that the priority among operators is a convenient, but not necessary, method of definition—the same information is conveyed by the hierarchical method of exposition.

The *term* provides a means of incorporating the multiplicative operators into arithmetic expressions and its forms are:

> Factor
> Term/factor
> Term∗factor

where "factor" is defined below. This definition effectively states that multiplicative operators in sequence are executed from left to right. Thus, for example, in the expression A∗B/C, the subexpression A∗B is executed first.

The *factor* provides a means of incorporating the exponentiation operator and its forms are:

> primary
> primary∗∗factor

where "primary" is defined below. This definition states that a factor is formed from a sequence of primaries separated by exponentiation operators. Thus, the exponentiation operator has the highest priority and is executed before operators with a lower priority, such as multiplication or addition. The definition also determines that successive exponentiation operators are executed from right to left, since "factor" is placed in the position of the rightmost operand. Thus, in the expression A∗∗B∗∗C, the subexpression B∗∗C is executed first, as though the expression were written A∗∗(B∗∗C).

A *primary* is the basic ingredient in an arithmetic expression and specifies the use of parentheses for grouping; its forms are:

Unsigned arithmetic constant

Arithmetic parameter
Arithmetic variable reference
Arithmetic array element reference
Arithmetic function reference
Arithmetic expression enclosed in parentheses

The above function rules also denote that there are no implied operators, as in "implied multiplication," and two operators may not appear in succession. Thus, an incorrect expression, such as A+-B, would have to be correctly written as A+(-B).

5.2.4 Special Arithmetic Expressions

Two special cases of arithmetic expressions may be used in FORTRAN 77: an arithmetic constant expression and an integer constant expression. An *arithmetic constant expression* is a valid arithmetic expression in which each primary, as defined previously, is either an arithmetic constant, an arithmetic parameter, or an arithmetic constant expression in parentheses. In this type of expression, exponentiation is not permitted unless the exponent has a value with an integer data type.

An *integer constant expression* is an arithmetic constant expression in which each arithmetic constant or arithmetic parameter is of type integer.

5.2.5 Evaluation Rules for Arithmetic Expressions

An arithmetic expression in its most simple or most sophisticated form has a data type. An arithmetic constant, for example, has a data type that is determined by the form in which the constant is written. Similarly, the data type of a variable, an element of an array, and a function reference is determined by the name of that entity. It follows, therefore, that the data type of an expression is determined by the data types of the operands and the functions that are referenced.

5.2.5.1 Single-Mode Expressions

A single-mode expression is one in which all operands are of the same data type. The data type of the value of a single-mode expression is the same as the data type of the operands.

5.2.5.2 Mixed-Mode Expressions

A mixed-mode expression is one that contains operands with two or more data types. In this case, the data type of the result of the expression is governed by conversion rules as they apply successively to the intermediate results generated during the evaluation of the expression. For example, the addition of a real operand and an integer operand generates a result with a data type of real. The conversion rules that apply to addition, subtraction, multiplication, and division in FORTRAN 77 are given in Table 5.2. The conversion operations contained therein need not be supplied by the programmer and are performed automatically by the processor. In the evaluation of the following sequence of statements, for example:

INTEGER I
REAL A,C,D
DOUBLE PRECISION B
D=I/(A+B)*(C+1.5)

the following actions would be performed:

1. Real variable A would be converted to double precision and added to B; the result would be double precision. Call it E. The resulting statement would then be:

D=I/E*(C+1.5)

2. Integer variable I would be converted to double precision and divided by E; the result would be double precision. Call it F. The resulting statement would then be:

D=F*(C+1.5)

3. Real variable C would be added to real constant 1.5; the result would be real. Call it G. The resulting statement would then be:

D=F*G

4. Intermediate real result G would then be converted to double precision and multipled by F; the result is double precision. Call it H. The resulting statement would then be:

D=H

TABLE 5.2 SUMMARY OF THE MANNER IN WHICH THE EXPRESSION $x_1 \oplus x_2$ IS EVALUATED FOR VARIOUS OPERAND TYPES, WHERE $\oplus$ IS +, −, *, or /†

x_1 \ x_2	I_2	R_2	D_2	C_2
I_1	$I=I_1 \oplus I_2$	$R=REAL(I_1) \oplus R_2$	$D=DBLE(I_1) \oplus D_2$	$C=CMPLX(REAL(I_1),0.) \oplus C_2$
R_1	$R=R_1 \oplus REAL(I_2)$	$R=R_1 \oplus R_2$	$D=DBLE(R_1) \oplus D_2$	$C=CMPLX(R_1,0.) \oplus C_2$
D_1	$D=D_1 \oplus DBLE(I_2)$	$D=D_1 \oplus DBLE(R_2)$	$D=D_1 \oplus D_2$	Prohibited
C_1	$C=C_1 \oplus CMPLX(REAL(I_2),0.)$	$C=C_1 \oplus CMPLX(R_2,0.)$	Prohibited	$C=C_1 \oplus C_2$

†(I denotes an integer operand, R denotes a real operand, D denotes a double precision operand, and C denotes a complex operand.)

5. For the assignment statement, which is covered later, the double precision result H of the expression would be converted to real and then stored in D to complete the execution of the statement.

5.2.5.3 Unary Operators

An operator with one operand is called a *unary operator*. As covered previously, there are two unary operators in FORTRAN 77: negation and identity, written –A and +A, respectively. The data type of the result of a unary operator is the same as the data type of the operand.

5.2.5.4 Integer Division

As shown in Table 5.2, the result of an integer division operation is a value of type integer. For example, the expression –5/2 would yield a result of –2. The integer quotient is computed according to the following rules:

1. If the magnitude of the mathematical quotient is less than one, then the result is zero. (For example, –1/3 yields 0 as does 1/2.)
2. If the magnitude of the mathematical quotient is greater than or equal to one, then the result is the largest integer with a value that does not exceed the magnitude of the mathematical quotient with an arithmetic sign that is the same as the sign of the mathematical quotient. (For example, (–10)/3 yields a result of (–3) and (–17)/(–5) yields a result of 3.)

5.2.5.5 Exponention

In general, the conversion rules denote that when an arithmetic operator is applied to operands of different data types, the operand that differs from the data type of the result is converted to the data type of the result so that the arithmetic operation is performed on operands of the same type. The exponentiation operator is the exception to this rule. As shown in Table 5.3, the integer operand is not converted when a real, double precision, or complex value is raised to an integer power.

For an integer value raised to an integer power, i.e., $I_1 ** I_2$, the value of the result is equal to $1/(I_1 ** ABS(I_2))$ when I_2 is negative, and the rules for integer quotients applies to the integer division.

TABLE 5.3   SUMMARY OF THE MANNER IN WHICH THE EXPRESSION $x_1 ** x_2$ IS EVALUATED FOR VARIOUS OPERAND TYPES†

x_1 \ x_2	I_2	R_2	D_2	C_2
I_1	$I=I_1**I_2$	$R=REAL(I_1)**R_2$	$D=DBLE(I_1)**D_2$	$C=CMPLX(REAL(I_1),0.)**C_2$
R_1	$R=R_1**I_2$	$R=R_1**R_2$	$D=DBLE(R_1)**D_2$	$C=CMPLX(R_1,0.)**C_2$
D_1	$D=D_1**I_2$	$D=D_1**DBLE(R_2)$	$D=D_1**D_2$	Prohibited
C_1	$C=C_1**I_2$	$C=C_1**CMPLX(R_2,0.)$	Prohibited	$C=C_1**C_2$

†(I denotes an integer operand, R denotes a real operand, D denotes a double precision operand, and C denotes a complex operand.)

5.3 CHARACTER EXPRESSIONS

A character expression represents a character-string value obtained through one or more concatenation operations on character values, the value of a character function, or as the value of a character constant, a character parameter, a character variable, or an element of a character array. Accordingly, the simplest form of a character expression is a character constant, a character parameter, a character variable reference, a character array reference, a character substring, or a character function reference. Through the use of the concatenation operator and parentheses, complex sequences of character-string operations can be specified.

5.3.1 Character Operators

One character operator is defined in FORTRAN 77: concatenation. The concatenation of two character operands c_1 and c_2 is specified as:

$$c_1 \; // \; c_2$$

and denotes the character value of c_1 concatenated on the right with the character value of c_2. Thus, the value of character expression 'ABC'//'123+' is the character string 'ABC123+'.

5.3.2 Character Operands

A character operand must specify a value of type character. The value used as an operand may be obtained from a character constant, a character parameter, a character variable, a character array reference, a character function reference, a character substring, or from the value of a sequence of character operations previously executed in the evaluation of the character expression. Since each of the ways of obtaining a character value constitutes a character expression, then it can be said that the operands to a concatenation operator must be character expressions.

5.3.3 Structure of Character Expressions

A hierarchy of definitions is used to specify the exact form of a character expression. The *character expression* exists at the highest level in the hierarchy and its forms are:

character primary
character expression // character primary

where "character primary," which is one of the operand forms given above, is defined more specifically below. This definition states that a character expression is either a character primary or is two or more character primaries separated by concatenation operators. The second form also denotes that successive concatenation operators are executed from left to right, so that $C//D//E$ is equivalent to $(C//D)//E$.

The *character primary* is the basic ingredient in a character expression and specifies the use of parentheses for grouping; its forms are:

character constant
character parameter
character variable reference
character array element reference
character substring reference
character function reference
character expression enclosed in parentheses

The above formation rules also denote that there is no implied concatenation operator, so that A B is simply interpreted as variable AB.

5.3.4 Special Character Expression

There is one special character expression in FORTRAN 77: a character constant expression. A *character constant expression* is a valid character expression in which the only permissible character primaries are character constants or character parameters.

5.4 RELATIONAL EXPRESSIONS

A relational expression represents a logical value* obtained through the comparison of two arithmetic expressions or through the comparison of two character expressions. A character expression may not be compared with an arithmetic expression. A relational expression may appear only in a logical expression. However, because a relational expression always yields a logical value, is by definition a logical expression. This topic is covered later.

*A logical value may assume a value of true or false.

5.4.1 Relational Operators

Six relational operators are defined in FORTRAN 77:

Operator	Name
.LT.	Less than
.LE.	Less than or equal to
.EQ.	Equal to
.NE.	Not equal to
.GE.	Greater than or equal to
.GT.	Greater than

Each operator requires two operands in the form:

$$x_1 \underline{\text{relop}} x_2$$

where x_1 and x_2 are both arithmetic or both character operands. The meanings of the six relational operators are given in Table 5.4.

TABLE 5.4   FORM AND MEANING OF RELATIONAL OPERATORS*

Form	Meaning
x_1 .LT. x_2	Less than: The value of the expression is true if the value of x_1 is less than the value of x_2. The value of the expression is false otherwise.
x_1 .LE. x_2	Less than or equal to: The value of the expression is true if the value of x_1 is less than or equal to the value of x_2. The value of the expression is false otherwise.
x_1 .EQ. x_2	Equal to: The value of the expression is true if the value of x_1 is equal to the value of x_2. The value of the expression is false otherwise.
x_1 .NE. x_2	Not equal to: The value of the expression is true if the value of x_1 is not equal to the value of x_2. The value of the expression is false otherwise.
x_1 .GE. x_2	Greater than or equal to: The value of the expression is true if the value of x_1 is greater than or equal to the value of x_2. The value of the expression is false otherwise.
x_1 .GT. x_2	Greater than: The value of the expression is true if the value of x_1 is greater than the value of x_2. The value of the expression is false otherwise.

*(x_1 are x_2 both arithmetic or both character expressions.)

5.4.2 Relational Operands

Operands to relational operators may be valid arithmetic or valid character expressions. The priority among FORTRAN 77 operators is such that arithmetic and character operators are executed before relational operators.

5.4.3 Evaluation of Relational Expressions

The value of a relational expression is either true or false. The manner in which the expression is evaluated is dependent upon the data type of the operands.

5.4.3.1 Arithmetic Relational Expressions

An arithmetic relational expression takes the form:

$$e_1 \text{ \underline{relop} } e_2$$

where e_1 and e_2 are arithmetic expressions of type integer, real, double precision, or complex, and *relop* is a relational operator. The operands e_1 and e_2 may have a complex data type only if the relational operator .EQ. or .NE. is used.

The result of an arithmetic relational expression has a true value if the specified relation holds. If the data types e_1 and e_2 differ, then the expression is evaluated as follows:

$$((e_1) - (e_2)) \text{ \underline{relop} } 0$$

where the rules for type conversion apply to the expression $((e_1) - (e_2))$ and the value 0 has the same data type as the evaluated expression. If the expression $((e_1) - (e_2))$ results in an invalid expression, then that form of comparison is not permitted. Thus, a complex expression may not be compared with a double precision expression.

5.4.3.2 Character Relational Expressions

With character operands, the character bit values of the operands are compared and the value of the relational expression is true if the stated conditional holds. The form of a character relational expression is:

$$c_1 \text{ \underline{relop} } c_2$$

where c_1 and c_2 are character expressions and *relop* is a relational operator.

The result of a character relational expression is dependent upon the character collating sequence. Thus, c_1 is less than c_2 if c_1 precedes c_2 in the collating sequence. However, tests for equality are not dependent upon the collating sequence, so that the operators .EQ. and .NE. may be used on any processor. The other relational operators are processor-dependent.

If the character operands are of differing lengths, a relational expression is evaluated as though the shorter operand were padded on the right with blank characters to the length of the longer operand.

5.5 LOGICAL EXPRESSIONS

A logical expression represents a logical value obtained through a logical computation or as the value of a logical constant, a logical parameter, a logical variable, or an element of a logical array. Accordingly, the simplest form of a logical expression is a logical constant, a logical parameter, a logical variable reference, a logical array reference, or a logical function reference.* Through the use of logical operators and parentheses, complex sequences of computations can be specified.

5.5.1 Logical Operators

Five logical operators are defined in FORTRAN 77:

Operator	Name
.NOT.	Logical negation
.AND.	Logical conjunction
.OR.	Logical inclusive disjunction
.EQV.	Logical equivalence
.NEQV.	Logical nonequivalence

The logical negation operator .NOT. is used with one operand; the .AND., .OR., .EQV., and .NEQV. operators require two operands.

The form and meaning of the five logical operators are given in Table 5.5   The interpretation of a logical expression is based on a

---

*A logical function reference may in itself require logical computations in the evaluation of its arguments and may specify logical computations in the body of the function.

TABLE 5.5 FORM AND MEANING OF LOGICAL OPERATORS*

x_1	x_2	.NOT. x_2	x_1 .AND. x_2	x_1 .OR. x_2	x_1 .EQV. x_2	x_1 .NEQV. x_2
true	true	false	true	true	true	false
true	false	true	false	true	false	true
false	true	false	false	true	false	true
false	false	true	false	false	true	false

*(x_1 and x_2 denote logical operands.)

precedence relation among the logical operators, which is listed as follows:

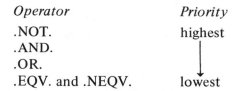

Operator	Priority
.NOT.	highest
.AND.	
.OR.	
.EQV. and .NEQV.	lowest

The precedence rules apply to sequential operators in an expression such that operators with a higher priority are executed before operators with a lower priority. Thus, in the expression:

Q .EQV. R .AND. S .OR. T

the operators are effectively executed in the following order:

1. R .AND. S Denote the result by A yielding Q .EQV. A .OR. T
2. A .OR. T Denote the result by B yielding Q .EQV. B
3. Q .EQV. B Giving the final result

Similarly, evaluation of the expression .NOT. U .AND. V, when U is false and V is true yields a true result, since the logical negation operator is executed first.

5.5.2 Logical Operands

Logical operands must specify values that have a logical data type. The value used as an operand may be obtained from a logical constant, a logical parameter, a logical variable, a logical array reference, a logical function reference, the result of a relational expression, or from the value of a sequence of operations previously executed in the evaluation of the logical expression. Since each of the ways of obtaining a logical value constitutes a logical expression, then it can be said that the operands to a logical operator must be logical expressions.

5.5.3 Structure of Logical Expressions

A hierarchy of definitions is used to specify the exact form of a logical expression. The hierarchy is suggested by Figure 5.2, which contains a pictorial representation of the form of a logical expression.

The *logical expression* exists at the highest level in the hierarchy and its forms are:

> logical disjunct
> logical expression .EQV. logical disjunct
> logical expression .NEQV. logical disjunct

where "logical disjunct" is defined below. This definition effectively states that in a logical expression containing two or more .EQV. or .NEQV. operators, the logical disjuncts are combined from left to right. (This is another way of saying that successive .EQV. and .NEQV. operators are executed from left to right.) Thus, in the expression U .EQV. V .NEQV. W, the operators are executed as though (U .EQV. V) .NEQV. W were written.

The *logical disjunct* provides a means of incorporating the logical disjunction operator which is .OR., and its forms are:

> logical term
> logical disjunct .OR. logical term

where "logical term" is defined below. This definition states that in a logical expression containing two or more .OR. operators, the logical terms are combined from left to right. (This is another way of saying that successive .OR. operators are executed from left to right.) Thus, in the expression A .OR. B .OR. C, the operators are executed as though (A .OR. B) .OR. C were written.

The *logical term* provides a means of incorporating the logical conjunction operator .AND., and its forms are:

> logical factor
> logical term .AND. logical factor

where "logical factor" is defined below. This definition states that in a logical expression containing two or more .AND. operators, the logical factors are combined from left to right. (This is another way

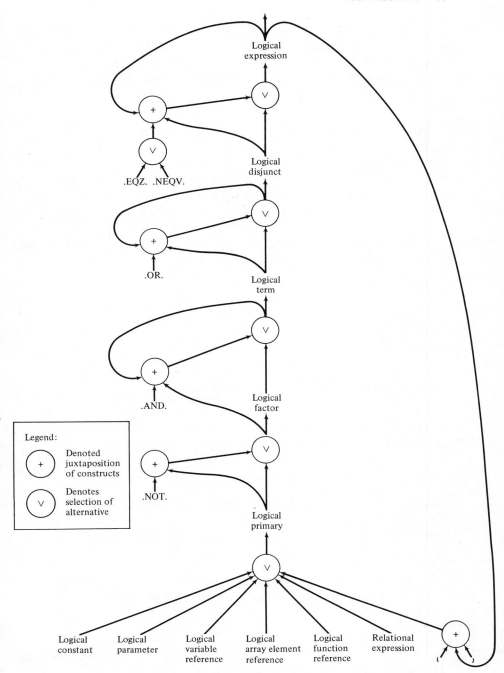

Figure 5.2   Pictorial representation of the form of a logical expression.

of saying that successive .AND. operators are executed from left to right.) Thus, in the expression I .AND. J .AND. K, the expression is executed as though (I .AND. J) .AND. K were written.

The *logical factor* is a means of incorporating the logical negation operator .NOT. and its forms are:

logical primary

.NOT. logical primary

where "logical primary" is defined below. Because .NOT. is placed lower in the hierarchical set of definitions, the .NOT. operator is executed before .AND., .OR., .EQV., or .NEQV.. Thus, in the expression .NOT. Q .OR. S .AND. T, the statement is executed as though (.NOT. Q) .OR. (S .AND. T) were written.

A *logical primary* is the basic ingredient in a logical expression and specifies the use of parentheses for grouping; its forms are:

logical constant
logical parameter
logical variable reference
logical array element reference
logical function reference
relational expression
logical expression enclosed in parentheses

As with previous types of expressions, the formation rules for logical expressions also denote that there are no implied logical operators and two logical operators may not appear in succession.

5.5.4 Special Logical Expressions

There is one special logical expression in FORTRAN 77: a logical constant expression. A *logical constant expression* is a valid logical expression in which each primary is one of the following:

logical constant
logical parameter
relational expression in which each primary is a constant
    expression
logical constant expression in parentheses

Thus, a logical constant expression may contain arithmetic and character constant expressions.

5.5.5 Note on the Execution of Logical Expressions

One of the rules of FORTRAN 77 is that it is not necessary for the processor to evaluate all operands of an operation or even execute all operators in an expression if the value of an expression can be determined otherwise. While this rule applies to the evaluation of all expressions, it is particularly applicable to logical expressions since the truth value of a logical expression is frequently based on the value of one operand. For example, in the expression

A .LT. B .OR. C .GT. D

only one true operand to the .OR. operator is needed to yield a true value for the expression. Therefore, if A is less than B, then there is no need to evaluate the subexpression C .GT. D and the value of the expression is true. Similarly, in the expression

A .GT. B .AND. C .LT. D

only one false operand is needed to the .AND. operator to yield a false value for the expression. Therefore, if A is not greater than B, then there is no need to evaluate the subexpression C .LT. D and the value of the expression is false.

5.6 INTERPRETATION AND EVALUATION OF EXPRESSIONS IN GENERAL

A variety of rules and operational conventions apply to the evaluation of expressions in general. The topics concern the priority of operators of different types, integrity of parentheses, interpretation rules, execution of functions, and rules that apply to specific types of expressions.

5.6.1 Priority of Operators of Different Types

When operators of different types, such as arithmetic, relational, and logical, appear in an expression, the following hierarchy exists among the various operators:

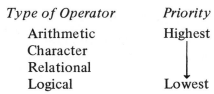

Type of Operator	*Priority*
Arithmetic	Highest
Character	
Relational	
Logical	Lowest

Therefore, in the expression A+B*C .LT. D .AND. Q, the operators are executed as though the expression ((A+(B*C)) .LT. D) .AND. Q were written. (It is assumed here that A,B,C, and D are arithmetic variables and Q is a logical variable.)

5.6.2 Integrity of Parentheses and Interpretation Rules

The use of parentheses plays a special role in FORTRAN 77, because in certain cases, the processor can use mathematical associative or distributive laws to reorder the execution of operators within an expression to minimize processing time. *However, expressions within parentheses must be treated as an entity.* Thus, the use of parentheses serves as a starting place for a summarization of rules for combining operators with operands:

1. Use of parentheses
2. Precedence of operators
3. Right to left interpretation of exponentiation operators in a factor
4. Left to right interpretation of multiplicative (multiplication or division) operators in a term
5. Left to right interpretation of additive (addition or subtraction) operators in an arithmetic expression
6. Left to right interpretation of concatenation operators in a character expression
7. Left to right interpretation of conjunction operators (i.e., .AND.) in a logical term
8. Left to right interpretation of disjunction operators (i.e., .OR.) in a logical disjunct
9. Left to right interpretation of logical equivalence operators (i.e., .EQV. or .NEQV.) in a logical expression

The relational operators and the logical negation operator (i.e., .NOT.) enter into the picture through item 2 – precedence of operators.

5.6.3 Mathematical Considerations

Some obvious and not so obvious considerations apply to the evaluation of expressions in FORTRAN 77. The obvious considerations are listed as follows:

1. An entity must be defined at the time when it is referenced and it must be defined with a value of the correct type.
2. An operation that is not defined mathematically, such as zero raised to the zero power, may not be used.

The "not so obvious" considerations concern mathematical equivalence. Two expressions are mathematically equivalent if for all values of their primaries, they produce equivalent results. Moreover, the distinction between integer division, for example, and real division is considered to be a mathematical difference. The processor may substitute equivalent mathematical forms during the interpretation of an expression, as covered below.

5.6.4 Function References

Some restrictions on the use of defined external functions are necessary to maintain the integrity of results generated by the processor. The restrictions do not apply to defined external functions in general, but to how a defined external function may be used in a given expression. The restrictions are listed as follows:

1. The execution of a function in an expression may not define any other entity that appears in the expression, either through the explicit assignment of a variable in the argument list or implicitly through common storage. Thus, for example, in the expression

$$A=B+FCN(B)+C(I)$$

   the function FCN must not affect the values of variables B or I or of the array C.

2. In statements that contain more than one function reference, the functions may be executed in any order, with the following exception:

   (a) When one function reference occurs in the argument list of another function reference, as in:

$$A=FCNA(B+FCNB(C))$$

   where FCNA and FCNB are functions. (Here, FCNB is executed before FCNA.)

   (b) When one function reference occurs in the logical expression part of a logical IF statement and another function reference occurs in the statement part of the same logical IF statement, as in:

IF(A .AND. FCNR(T)) A=B+FCNB(C)

where FCNR and FCNB are functions. (Here, FCNR is executed before FCNB.)

The net result of the above restrictions on function references is that one function reference may not define a variable that would affect the value of any other function reference in the same expression, except for the logical IF statement as mentioned above.

5.6.5 Evaluation of Expressions

The rule given above that "it is not necessary for a processor to evaluate all operands in an expression if the value of the expression can be determined otherwise" is amplified here through specific consideration of arguments, subscripts, substring references, arithmetic expressions, relational expressions, logical expressions, and character expressions.

5.6.5.1 Arguments

The data type of an expression containing a function reference is independent of the data type of an expression that constitutes an actual argument in the argument list of the function. Thus, the data type of the expression does not affect the data type of the actual argument and similarly, the data type of the actual argument does not affect the data type of the expression containing the function reference.

5.6.5.2 Subscripts

The data type of a subscript in an expression containing an array reference is independent of the data type of the expression. Thus, the data type of a subscript expression does not affect the data type of the expression containing the corresponding array reference, and the data type of an expression does not affect the evaluation of a subscript corresponding to an array reference in the expression.

5.6.5.3 Substring References

The evaluation of the integer expressions that comprise a character substring reference are independent of the character expression in which they are imbedded.

5.6.5.4 Mathematical Equivalence

A processor is permitted to substitute a mathematically equivalent form in the evaluation of an expression provided that the integrity of parentheses is maintained and that integer operands are not combined with other operands so as to yield a result that is not equivalent. Tables 5.6 and 5.7 give allowable and nonallowable forms, respectively.

TABLE 5.6 ALLOWABLE ALTERNATE FORMS FOR ARITHMETIC EXPRESSIONS[†]

Expression	Allowable Alternate Form
A+B	B+A
A*B	B*A
−A+B	B−A
A+B+C	A+(B+C)
A−B+C	A−(B−C)
A*B/C	A*(B/C)
A*B−A*C	A*(B−C)
A/B/C	A/(B*C)
A/5.0	0.2*A

[†]Note: A, B, and C are real, double precision, or complex operands.

TABLE 5.7 NONALLOWABLE FORMS FOR ARITHMETIC EXPRESSIONS[†]

Expression	Nonallowable Alternate Form	Reason
I/2	0.5*I	Different mathematical form
A*I/J	A*(I/J)	Different mathematical form
I/J/A	I/(J*A)	Different mathematical form
(A*B)−(A*C)	A*(B−C)	Integrity of parentheses
A*(B−C)	A*B−A*C	Integrity of parentheses

[†]Note: A,B, and C are real, double precision, or complex operands. I and J are integer operands.

5.6.5.5 Relational Equivalence

Two relational expressions are equivalent if their logical values are equal for all possible values of their primaries. Thus, for example, in the relational expression A .GT. B, the processor may select the method of evaluation as B−A .LT. 0.0 provided that the rules given previously for the evaluation of relational expressions are satisfied.

5.6.5.6 Logical Equivalence

Two logical expressions are equivalent if their logical values are equal for all possible values of their primaries. Therefore, the processor may select an alternate form for evaluation provided that it is logically equivalent. The following examples demonstrate the above concepts for logical variable P, Q, and R:

Expression	Alternate Form	Comment
P .AND. Q .AND. R	P .AND. (Q .AND. R)	OK—logically equivalent
(P .AND. Q) .AND. R	P .AND. (Q .AND. R)	Not OK—integrity of parentheses violated.

In all cases, the rules given previously for the evaluation of logical expressions and the evaluation of operands continue to apply.

5.6.5.7 Character Expressions

The rule given previously for the evaluation of operands also applies to character expressions. Consider the following example in which the length of character variables C, D, and E is two characters and CFCN is a function that returns a character value:

$$\text{CHARACTER}*2 \text{ C,D,E,CFCN}$$
$$\text{C=D//CFCN(E)}$$

In this case, it is not necessary to evaluate the function CFCN since the assignment operation for variable C is determined solely by variable D, since both have a character length of two.

6 | EXECUTION AND CLASSIFICATION OF FORTRAN STATEMENTS

6.1 OBJECTIVE OF THE CLASSIFICATION

The purpose of this chapter is to describe the execution sequence of statements in a FORTRAN 77 program, to distinguish between executable and nonexecutable statements, and to delineate the various types of statements. This chapter serves as a prelude to successive chapters that cover the individual statements in FORTRAN 77.

6.2 EXECUTION SEQUENCE

The *execution sequence* in FORTRAN 77 programs is defined as the order in which statements are executed by the processor. Three aspects are considered: normal execution sequence, transfer of control, and miscellaneous considerations.

6.2.1 Normal Execution Sequence

The normal sequence in which statements are executed in a FORTRAN 77 program is the order in which the statements appear in a main program or in an external procedure. Execution of an executable program begins with the first executable statement in the main program, and normal execution sequence continues from there.

When an external procedure is referenced in a main program or an external procedure, execution of the calling statement is suspended and execution continues with the first executable statement in the called procedure that immediately follows the corresponding FUNCTION, SUBROUTINE, or ENTRY statement. Execution is returned from the called procedure to the calling statement through an explicit or implicit return statement, and normal execution continues from where it was suspended or from an alternate point in the calling program.

Execution of an executable program is terminated normally by the processor when a STOP statement is executed in the main program or an external procedure, or an END statement is executed in the main program. The execution of an executable program is terminated abnormally by the processor when an operational condition occurs that prevents further execution.

6.2.2 Transfer of Control

The normal execution sequence may be altered through the execution of one of several FORTRAN 77 statements that causes the normal execution sequence to be discontinued and causes execution to resume at a specified statement in a main program or external procedure. Statements that can be used to cause a transfer of control to take place are:

1. GO TO statement
2. Arithmetic IF statement
3. RETURN and STOP statements
4. An input/output statement through the error and end-of-file specifiers
5. CALL statement
6. Logical IF statement that includes one of the above statements
7. Block IF and ELSE IF statements
8. DO statement
9. END statement

The last statement in an IF block or an ELSE IF block or the terminal statement in a DO loop also implicitly cause a transfer of control through the control mechanism inherent in these structures.

Each of the above statements is described in subsequent chapters.

6.2.3 Miscellaneous Considerations

The execution sequence of FORTRAN 77 programs is not affected by nonexecutable statements and comment lines, and recursive procedures are not permitted. Once an external procedure has been referenced, the same procedure must not be again referenced before the execution of a RETURN or END statement corresponding to the prior reference to that procedure.

6.3 EXECUTABLE AND NONEXECUTABLE STATEMENTS

FORTRAN 77 statements are classified by whether they are executable or nonexecutable. An executable statement performs an identifiable function in an executable program and exists as a part of a path of statements that comprise a possible execution sequence. A nonexecutable statement specifies information to the processor that governs the execution of the program. Both executable and nonexecutable statements may be assigned a statement number; however, transfer of control may not be directed to a nonexecutable statement through its statement number.

6.3.1 List of Executable Statements

Executable statements perform computational, control, and input/output related functions and are listed and delineated as follows:

Statement	*Major Function or Qualification*
Assignment	Allows computations to be performed and values of variables or arrays to be defined. Statement numbers may be ASSIGNed to integer variables.
GO TO	Transfer of control on an unconditional, assigned, or computed basis.
IF	Conditional branching or statement execution based on the value of an arithmetic or logical expression, respectively.
Block IF	Provides an IF-THEN-ELSE facility for conditional statement execution.

STOP and PAUSE	Provides the facility for termination of the execution of an executable program or temporary suspension of an executable program.
DO	Provides a facility for controlling program looping.
CONTINUE	Provides a statement that performs no operational function but can be used with a statement number to serve as a point of reference in a program unit.
READ, WRITE, and PRINT	Provide input and output functions.
REWIND, BACKSPACE, ENDFILE, OPEN, CLOSE, and INQUIRE	Provide input/output control facilities.
CALL and RETURN	Cause invocation of and return from an external procedure.
END	Used as the physical end of a program unit and causes program termination or return to the calling program when executed by the processor in a main program or external procedure, respectively.

The executable statements are organized into three classes: assignment, control, and input/output.

6.3.2 List of Nonexecutable Statements

Nonexecutable statements are not used to form an execution sequence and are listed and delineated as follows:

Statement	*Major Function or Qualification*
PROGRAM, FUNCTION, SUBROUTINE, ENTRY, and BLOCK DATA	Identifies the beginning of a program unit, allows it to be named, and permits control information to be specified.
DIMENSION, COMMON,	Permits storage management re-

EQUIVALENCE, IMPLICIT, PARAMETER, EXTERNAL, INTRINSIC, and SAVE	quirements to be established and symbolic names to be specified.
INTEGER, REAL, DOUBLE PRECISION, COMPLEX, LOGICAL, and CHARACTER	Permit data types and storage requirements to be specified.
DATA	Allows data values to be set prior to program execution.
FORMAT	Allows information that controls input and output editing to be specified.
Statement function	Allows a one-statement internal function to be defined.

The nonexecutable statements are organized into three classes: specification, format specifications, and subprograms.

7 | SPECIFICATION STATEMENTS

7.1 OVERVIEW

Collectively, specification statements provide information to the processor on how storage should be managed, how symbolic names should be interpreted and used, and how statements should be executed. Specification statements are most frequently used to establish data types and storage requirements and this topic is covered first. Afterwards, the specification statements are grouped in general by the kind of information for which they can be used to provide information to the processor.

7.2 TYPE STATEMENTS

A type statement can be used to establish the data type of an entity by overriding implicit type specifications and to specify the dimension of arrays. When a symbolic name appears in a type statement, the data type of the corresponding entity is thereby established for all occurrences of that name in the program unit in which it is declared. A symbolic name may only appear in one type statement. The symbolic name of a main program, subroutine subprogram, or a block data program unit may not appear in a type statement. The data type of the following entities may be specified in a type statement: variable, parameter, array, function, or dummy procedure name. A type statement may also be used to confirm implicit typing for purposes of documentation.

7.2.1 Arithmetic Type Statement

The form of an arithmetic type statement is:

$$typ \; v[,v] \ldots$$

where *typ* is INTEGER, REAL, DOUBLE PRECISION, COMPLEX, or LOGICAL, and *v* is a variable name, parameter name, array name, array declarator, function name, or dummy procedure name. The type statement declares the specified entities to have the corresponding data type. That is, the INTEGER statement is used to declare entities of type integer, the REAL statement is used to declare entities of type REAL, etc. Thus, in the following statements:

```
INTEGER ACAT,I3,FOR(3,-1:5)
REAL J, SUM(-5:30),DIFF(3,8,5),QTE
DOUBLE PRECISION IDENT,RSLT(100)
LOGICAL Q,R(0:10,5),TLIST,PFLAG
COMPLEX OHM(6,-10:10,1,10),BXER
```

the following declarations are made:

1. ACAT and I3 are integer names; FOX is an integer array. (The specification of I3 is a confirmation of implicit typing.)
2. J and QTE are real names; SUM and DIFF are real arrays. (The specification of QTE is a confirmation of implicit typing.)
3. IDENT is a double precision name; RSLT is a double precision array.
4. Q, TLIST, and PFLAG are logical names; R is a logical array.
5. BXER is a complex name; OHM is a complex array.

The subject of array declarators was covered in Chapter Four.

7.2.2 Character Type Statement

The form of a character type statement is:

$$\text{CHARACTER}[*len[,]] \; nam[,nam] \ldots$$

where *len* is a length specification that gives the length in number of characters of a character variable, element of a character array, character parameter, result of a character function reference, and *nam* is one of the following:

$$v[*len]$$
$$a[(d)]\ [*len]$$

where *v* is a symbolic name of one of the following: variable, parameter, function or dummy procedure; *a* is an array name, and *a(d)* is an array declarator.

The *length specification* can be an unsigned integer constant, a positive valued integer constant expression in parentheses, or an asterisk in parentheses.

The length specification following the keyword CHARACTER denotes the length of each entity in the statement that does not have its own length specification. Thus, in the following statement:

CHARACTER *4 LIST, PREFIX *1, TBLE(100)*8

the following character declarations are made:

LIST has a length specification of 4
PREFIX has a length specification of 1
TABLE has a length specification of 8

A length specification immediately following an entity applies only to that entity. When an array is declared, the length applies to *each* element in the declared array. If no length specification is given, as in:

CHARACTER A,B

a length of one is assumed.

The length specifier of (*) denotes that the length is to be determined in another way, and only applies to external function names, dummy arguments to an external procedure, and a character parameter. Otherwise, the length specification must be present in the form of a positive integer constant or an integer expression enclosed in parentheses with a positive value. In the case of a parameter, as in:

CHARACTER SFFX*(*)
PARAMETER(SFFX='AUGUST')

the length SFFX is picked up from the data value in the PARAMETER statement, which is 6 in this example. In the case of a declaration of a dummy argument in the definition of an external procedure, as in:

> CHARACTER FUNCTION DELETE(A)
> CHARACTER A*(*)
> . . .

the length of the argument, which is A in this example, is picked up as the length of the actual argument when the procedure is invoked. If the actual argument is an array name then the length that is picked up is the length of an element of the array. In the case of the name in an external function definition, as in:

> CHARACTER *(*) FUNCTION FILLUP(A,B)

the length of the function name, which is FILLUP in this example, is determined from the length that is specified in the program unit in which a reference to it occurs.

If an actual length specification is declared for an external function in the referencing program unit and in the function definition, the length specifications must agree or the function definition must use the (*) as covered above. The length specification for a character statement function or for a dummy argument in a character statement function must always be a positive integer constant or a positive value integer constant expression.

7.2.3 Comments on the Use of Type Statements

As mentioned in Chapter Two, type statements must be placed in the beginning of a program unit, but can be preceded by an IMPLICIT statement. The scope of symbolic names, including those declared in type statements, is the program unit in which they are included.

More than one type statement beginning with the same keyword may be included in a program unit. Thus, the statements:

> REAL Y12(100),IDENT,BOY(-5:5)
> LOGICAL Q,R,S
> REAL PARTNO(50,2)

are equivalent to:

> REAL Y12(100),IDENT,BOY(-5:5),PARTNO(50,2)
> LOGICAL Q,R,S

Array declarations may also be made with the DIMENSION statement.

7.3 SPECIFICATION STATEMENTS RELATED TO IMPLICIT NAMING, CONSTANT VALUES, AND ARRAY DECLARATIONS

Three statements can be placed in this category: the IMPLICIT statement, the PARAMETER statement, and the DIMENSION statement. The IMPLICIT statement can be used to change or confirm the default implicit typing for real and integer names and to establish implicit typing for other types of names. The PARAMETER statement can be used to give a symbolic name to a constant value. The DIMENSION statement can be used to declare an array and specify its dimensions.

7.3.1 The IMPLICIT Statement

The form of the IMPLICIT statement is:

IMPLICIT *typ*(a[,a] . . .) [,*typ*(a[,a] . . .)] . . .

where *typ* is one of the following keywords:

> INTEGER
> REAL
> DOUBLE PRECISION
> COMPLEX
> LOGICAL
> CHARACTER[*len*]

specifying a data type, and *a* is either a single alphabetic character or a range of alphabetic characters separated by a minus sign. For example, the statement

IMPLICIT INTEGER(A,X–Z),REAL(W),DOUBLE PRECISION
(B–H, O–V)

specifies integer implicit typing for symbolic names beginning with A and for names beginning with the letters X through Z, real implicit typing for symbolic names beginning with W, and double precision implicit typing for symbolic names beginning with B through H and O through V.

The attribute *len* for the keyword CHARACTER denotes a length specification, exactly as in the type statements covered above. For example, the following statement:

IMPLICIT CHARACTER *8(C)

specifies implicit typing for symbolic names beginning with the letter C to have a data type of CHARACTER with a length specification of 8.

An implicit type specification applies only to the program unit in which it is made, and can be overridden by a type statement or a FUNCTION statement for the same subprogram. An IMPLICIT statement must precede all other specification statements, except the PARAMETER statement, and cannot be used to override the type of intrinsic functions.

Two or more IMPLICIT statements may appear in a program unit, but a single letter may appear only once corresponding to an implicit type specification.

7.3.2 The PARAMETER Statement

The form of the PARAMETER statement is:

PARAMETER($p=e$ [,$p=e$] . . .)

where p is a symbolic name and e is a constant expression.* The symbolic name (p) and constant expression (e) must agree with regard to data type, subject to the following considerations:

1. If the type of p is arithmetic, then e must be an arithmetic constant expression.
2. If the type of p is logical, then e must be a logical constant expression.
3. If the type of p is character, then e must be a character constant expression.
4. If a parameter is used in the constant expression, it must be previously defined in a preceding PARAMETER statement or in the same PARAMETER statement.
5. The value of e is assigned to parameter p according to the rules established for the assignment statement, which is covered in Chapter Eight.

*Recall that a constant value is a primary that satisfies the definition of a constant expression.

6. A parameter must only be defined once in a program unit and that definition must be in a PARAMETER statement.

7. The data type of a parameter must be explicitly declared in a type statement or be implicitly implied through the use of an IMPLICIT statement, if a default implied type is not to be assumed for that symbolic name. The type declaration, either explicit or implicit, must precede the PARAMETER statement.

8. Character parameters require a length specification in a CHAR-ACTER or an IMPLICIT statement, if a length attribute other than 1 is desired.

The scope of a parameter is the program unit in which it is declared. After a parameter has been defined, it can be used as a primary in an expression and in a DATA statement. A parameter may not be used to form a complex constant. The following examples demonstrate the use of the parameter statement:

```
CHARACTER NAME*(*),PREFIX*3
LOGICAL Q
PARAMETER (NAME='ABC CORP',PREFIX='TLT',
    PI=3.141592818,LINES=56,Q=.FALSE.)
```

A constant and a parameter are not in general interchangeable. A parameter may only be used where it is explicitly stated that it can be used—such as a primary in an expression or in a DATA statement. A parameter may not be used, for example, to denote a character constant in a FORMAT statement.

7.3.3 The DIMENSION Statement

The form of a DIMENSION statement is:

DIMENSION $a(d)[,a(d)]$ . . .

where $a(d)$ is an array declarator as described in Chapter Four. Although a declaration of an array can appear only once in a program unit, an array declared in a DIMENSION statement may also have its name appear without dimensioning information in a type statement or a COMMON statement. The following are valid array declarations:

DIMENSION A(0:99), LIST(50,2,-10:10)

Dimensioning information for arrays may be specific as array declarators in type and COMMON statements.

7.4 STORAGE MANAGEMENT

Two statements are available in FORTRAN 77 that facilitate storage management between program units and within a program unit. The COMMON statement permits a block of storage to be shared between program units. The EQUIVALENCE statement permits different symbolic names to be associated with the same physical storage.

7.4.1 Common Storage

A storage sequence, composed of a succession of storage units, that is shared between program units is referred to as *common storage*. The concept works as follows:

1. A common area of storage that can be accessed by two or more program units is established with the COMMON statement.
2. Variables and arrays are assigned to the common area through their placement in the COMMON statement.
3. The variables and arrays, declared to be in common storage, become associated through their specification in the COMMON statement in each of their respective program units.

Through the use of common storage, the following capabilities are available:

1. The storage space required for larger tables or arrays can be shared among several program units instead of including the table or array in each program unit. Thus, storage can be utilized more effectively.
2. Large amounts of data can be passed from a calling program to a subprogram without having to use extensive parameter lists. Thus, the linking process is more efficient. Data in common storage can be visualized through a storage map.
3. The use of common storage allows good program organization and is convenient for the programmer.

7.4.1.1 Static and Dynamic Storage

Static storage refers to storage that is assigned to an executable program by an operating system when execution of the program is initiated and the storage remains assigned for the duration of program execution. *Dynamic storage* refers to storage that is allocated when a block is entered and is deallocated (or freed) when an exit is made from the block. In FORTRAN 77, storage that is assigned to the main program by the operating system for variables and arrays is static. Storage allocated in external subprograms (i.e., functions and subroutines) is dynamic, unless specified otherwise with the SAVE statement.

7.4.1.2 Types of Common Storage

Two types of common storage exist in FORTRAN 77; blank and labeled. *Blank common* is accessible by all program units in which it is declared and is statically defined. Blank common has no identifying symbolic name and one blank common area exists for the complete executable program. *Labeled common* is identified by a symbolic name and is accessible by all program units in which common storage with the same name is declared. Labeled common may be statically defined or dynamically defined, depending upon where it is declared.

If labeled common is declared in the main program, then it remains allocated for the duration of program execution. If labeled common is declared in a subprogram but not its calling program, then that labeled common block is allocated when the subprogram is entered and freed when an exit is made from the subprogram. A labeled common block allocated in a program unit remains allocated during subordinate calls and returns.

Figure 7.1 gives the structure of a sample program that uses common storage. The executable program is composed of program units A through G, with A being the main program. The operational structure of the program is as follows:

1. A can invoke B or C.
2. B can invoke D or E.
3. C can invoke F or G.

Figure 7.1 also gives common blocks that are declared in program units A through G. Blank common and labeled common block ALBL are defined in A and are thereby accessible to all program units that declare them. As a results, program units B, D, and F can access blank common and program units E and G can access labeled common block ALBL. Program unit B declares labeled common

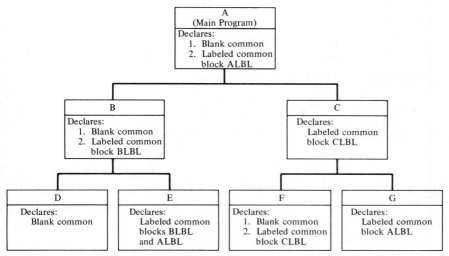

Figure 7.1 Structure of a sample program that uses common storage.

block BLBL, which is potentially accessible by program units D and E. As a result, program unit E can access labeled common block BLBL because it declares that common block. Program unit C declares labeled common block CLBL, which is potentially accessible by program units F and G. As a result, program unit F can access labeled common block CLBL because it declares that common block.

7.4.1.3 The COMMON Statement

The form of the COMMON statement is:

COMMON [/[cb]/]nlist[[,]/[cb]/nlist] . . .

where *cb* is the symbolic name of a common block, and *nlist* is a list of variable names, array names, and array declarators. A given symbolic name may appear only once in one COMMON statement. Dummy argument and function names may not appear in a COMMON statement. If the common block name is omitted, then blank common is indicated. If the common block name is omitted from the first block specified in a COMMON statement, then the enclosing slashes may also be omitted. The *nlist* that follows a common block name indicates the data elements that are to be organized in that common block. For example, in the statement:

COMMON A,B(5,5)/DBASE/NAME,ADDR,AGE/DLIST/
N,WORK(15),PAY(15)

the following common storage assignments are made:

A and B are placed in blank common
NAME, ADDR, and AGE are placed in common block DBASE
N, WORK, and PAY are placed in common block DLIST

Variables and arrays in a common block are placed in common storage in the order specified in the COMMON statement. The variable and array names need not be the same in the program units referencing the same common block; however, the entries must agree in order, type, and number.

Two successive slashes indicate blank common. For example, in the statements

COMMON A,B/ALBL/C,D//E,F
COMMON /ALBL/G,H//I,J

variables A,B,E,F,I, and J are placed in blank common in the order given. Variables C,D,G, and H are placed in common block labeled ALBL in the order given. The list of variable names or arrays following each successive appearance of a common block name is interpreted as a continuation of the preceding common block declaration.

7.4.1.4 Storage of Common Blocks

A common block is comprised of a sequence of storage units consisting of the storage units of entities in the list of variables and arrays for that common block, organized in the order written in the COMMON statement. The number of storage units needed to store a common block are referred to as its size.

In an executable program, all labeled common blocks, declared in various program units, with the same name must have the same size. Blank common blocks declared in various program units of an executable program need not have the same size.

In an executable program, all common blocks with the same name have the same first storage unit, thereby establishing the association of data values between program units.

If a character variable or array is placed in a common block, then that block must be comprised of only character data.

A named common block may become undefined through the execution of an explicit or implicit return from an external procedure together with the dynamic storage properties of FORTRAN 77. However, the same conditions do not cause blank common to become undefined. Entities in a labeled common block may be initially defined with the DATA initialization statement. However, entities in blank common may *not* be initialized with the DATA statement.

7.4.2 Storage Equivalence

The EQUIVALENCE statement permits the association of variables and arrays that share storage units. This feature allows the same information to be referenced in different ways and facilitates programming when two or more persons collaborate. The EQUIVALENCE statement applies to entities in the same program unit.

7.4.2.1 The EQUIVALENCE Statement

The form of the EQUIVALENCE statement is:

EQUIVALENCE (*nlist*)[, (*nlist*)] . . .

where *nlist* is a list of variable names, array element names, array names, and character substring names. Any expression used in a subscript or substring designator must be an integer constant expression. For example, the statements:

REAL C(5),D(6)
EQUIVALENCE (C,D(2))

establish the following association:

$$C(1) \quad C(2) \quad C(3) \quad C(4) \quad C(5)$$
$$\updownarrow \qquad \updownarrow \qquad \updownarrow \qquad \updownarrow \qquad \updownarrow$$
$$D(1) \quad D(2) \quad D(3) \quad D(4) \quad D(5) \quad D(6)$$

The affect of the EQUIVALENCE statement is to provide association between the storage sequences occupied by entities whose names appear in the EQUIVALENCE statement. More specifically, the association is made between the first storage units of the elements in the EQUIVALENCE statement, so that the statement may cause the association of other elements as well. The affect of the EQUIVALENCE statement is only to provide association of storage units, and the statement has no affect on data types and data structures.

Dummy argument names and function names may not appear in an EQUIVALENCE statement.

If an array name appears in an EQUIVALENCE statement then the association is the same as if the first element in the array were specified. If an array element is specified in an EQUIVALENCE statement, the number of subscript expressions must equal the number of dimensions declared for that array.

7.4.2.2 Rules Governing the Use of the EQUIVALENCE Statement

Use of the EQUIVALENCE statement may not specify an arrangement of storage units that is physically impossible. The following cases fall into this category:

1. An EQUIVALENCE statement may not specify that the same storage unit may appear more than once in a storage sequence, as in

   REAL X(3),Y
   EQUIVALENCE (X (2),Y), (X(3),Y)

2. An EQUIVALENCE statement may not specify that consecutive storage units are to occupy nonconsecutive storage positions, as in:

   REAL X(2)
   COMPLEX Y (2)
   EQUIVALENCE (X(1),Y(1)), (X(2),Y(2))

In addition, use of the EQUIVALENCE statement must not specify a logical inconsistency, such as the association of two distinct common blocks.

7.4.2.3 Equivalence and Common Storage

Variables and arrays may be associated with entities in common storage, as in the following example:

> COMMON A,B,C(5)
> REAL D(7)
> EQUIVALENCE (A,D(1))

so that the following storage equivalence is established:

A	B	C(1)	C(2)	C(3)	C(4)	C(5)
↕	↕	↕	↕	↕	↕	↕
D(1)	D(2)	D(3)	D(4)	D(5)	D(6)	D(7)

and that the corresponding storage units are assigned from common storage.

The result of the EQUIVALENCE statement on the association of variables and arrays in common storage may be to lengthen the common block, as demonstrated in the following example:

> REAL A(8)
> COMMON C(2),B,D(3)
> EQUIVALENCE (C(1),A(1))

so that the common storage block is organized as follows:

A(1)	A(2)	A(3)	A(4)	A(5)	A(6)	A(7)	A(8)
↕	↕	↕	↕	↕	↕	↕	↕
C(1)	C(2)	B	D(1)	D(2)	D(3)	*	*

and where the asterisk (*) denotes a position at which the common block is lengthened. However, association through the use of the EQUIVALENCE statement may not cause common storage to be lengthened by adding storage units preceding the first storage unit in the common block. The following sequence of statements:

> COMMON /LST/I
> INTEGER K(3)
> EQUIVALENCE (I,K(2))

for example, demonstrate an incorrect storage assignment and are not allowed.

7.4.2.4 Character Equivalence

Character strings may be associated through equivalence only with other character strings. The character strings may be specified as character variables, character array names, character array element names, and character substring names. The association is made between the first storage units occupied by entities appearing in an equivalence list in an EQUIVALENCE statement, so that the statement may cause the association of other character elements as well. The following example of character equivalence:

CHARACTER A*8,B(3)*2,C*3
EQUIVALENCE (A(2:7),B(1)),(B(2),C)

can be depicted as follows:

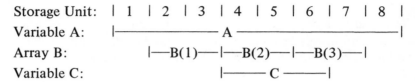

7.4.2.5 Association of Arrays

The 1966 FORTRAN standard permitted an n-dimensional array to be specified as a one-dimensional array for equivalence purposes. This has been changed in FORTRAN 77.

In FORTRAN 77, the interpretation of a one-dimensional subscript in an EQUIVALENCE list for an n-dimensional array is as though the subscript expression were the leftmost one and the missing subscript expressions each had their respective lower dimension bound value.

Table 7.1 gives formulas for converting a 1966 FORTRAN one-

TABLE 7.1   FORMULA FOR CONVERTING A 1966
FORTRAN ONE-DIMENSIONAL SUB-
SCRIPT IN AN EQUIVALENCE LIST
TO AN n-DIMENSIONAL SUBSCRIPT

n	Dimension	Subscript Value	Subscript
1	(d_1)	s	(s)
2	(d_1,d_2)	s	$(1+MOD(s-1,d_1),$ $1+(s-1)/d_1)$
3	(d_1,d_2,d_3)	s	$(1+MOD(s-1,d_1),$ $1+MOD((s-1)/d_1,d_2),$ $1+(s-1)/(d_1*d_2))$

dimensional subscript to the corresponding n-dimensional subscript. As an illustration, consider the following example:

1966 FORTRAN	*FORTRAN 77*
REAL A(3,4)	REAL A(3,4)
EQUIVALENCE (A(6),B)	EQUIVALENCE (A(3,2),B)

Using Table 7.1, the subscript for array A is computed as (1+MOD (5,3), 1+(5)/3), which yields (3,2). The formulae utilize the fact that arrays are stored in column order.

7.4.2.6 Partial Association

Two storage sequences* are *associated* if their respective storage units coincide. This means that the ith storage unit of the first storage sequence is the same as the jth storage unit of the second storage sequence, and that the $(i+k)^{th}$ storage unit of the first storage sequence is the same as the $(j+k)^{th}$ storage unit of the second storage sequence, for all k such that the $(i+k)^{th}$ and the $(j+k)^{th}$ characters are within their respective storage sequences.

Two associated entities are *totally associated* if their respective storage sequences are associated and are *partially associated*, otherwise. Through the following statement:

```
COMPLEX A(3)
REAL B(4),C
DOUBLE PRECISION D
EQUIVALENCE (A(2),B(2)),(B(1),C,D)
```

the storage association is depicted as:

```
Storage unit: |  1  |  2  |  3  |  4  |  5  |  6  |
Array A:      |———A(1)———|———A(2)———|———A(3)———|
Array B:          |—B(1)—|—B(2)—|—B(3)—|—B(4)—|
Variable C:       |—C—|
Variable D:       |———D———|
```

In this case, only B(1) and C are totally associated. All other associations are partial. For example, A(1) is partially associated with

*See Chapter One for a definition of storage sequence.

TABLE 7.2   METHODS FOR COMPUTING AN ARRAY INDEX

Number of Dimensions	Dimension Declarator	Dimensional Extent	Subscript Value	Array Index
1	$(j_1:k_1)$	d_1	s_1	$1+(s_1-j_1)$
2	$(j_1:k_1,j_2:k_2)$	d_1,d_2	(s_1,s_2)	$1+(s_1-j_1)+(s_2-j_2)*d_1$
3	$(j_1:k_1,j_2:k_2,j_3:k_3)$	d_1,d_2,d_3	(s_1,s_2,s_3)	$1+(s_1-j_1)+(s_2-j_2)*d_1$ $+(s_3-j_3)*d_2*d_1$
.				
.				
.				
n	$(j_1:k_1,\ldots,j_n:k_n)$	$d_1,\ldots,d_n$	$(s_1,\ldots,s_n)$	$1+(s_1-j_1)$ $+(s_2-j_2)*d_1$ $+(s_3-j_3)*d_2*d_1$ $+\ldots$ $+(s_n-j_n)*d_{n-1}$ $*d_{n-2}*\ldots*d_1$

Note: $d_i=k_i-j_i+1$

B(1), C, and D; A(2) is partially associated with B(2), B(3), and D; etc.

The concept of association applies to the effect of the EQUIVA-LENCE statement within a program unit and to the effect of the COMMON statement between program units.

7.4.3 Array Indexing

An item of information related to storage management involves the processing necessary to index into an array. Regardless of the number of dimensions and bounds, the elements of an array are ordered by column in a storage sequence and constitute a sequence of data elements. During program execution, the processor always maps a subscript value into an array index, prior to referencing the corresponding array element.

Table 7.2 gives a set of formulae for computing an array index.

7.5 DATA INITIALIZATION

Variables and array elements can be initialized when an executable program is loaded through the use of the DATA statement. Data entities not initialized with a DATA statement are undefined when a program begins execution and must be subsequently defined before they can be referenced.*

7.5.1 The DATA Statement

The form of the DATA statement is:

$$\text{DATA } nlist/clist/[[,] \; nlist/clist/] \ldots$$

where:

nlist is a list of variable names, array names, array element names, substring names, and implied-DO lists, and

clist is a constant list of the form

$a[,a] \ldots$

where each a is either a constant or a parameter or a repetition factor of the form $n*$ followed by a constant or parameter, denoting n successive appearances of the constant or parameter separated by commas. For example, 4∗3.14 would be equivalent to the list: 3.14, 3.14, 3.14, 3.14.

An example of a DATA statement would be:

```
REAL A(3),B
INTEGER R,I(4),P
CHARACTER *4 LIST(3)
LOGICAL Q
COMPLEX C
PARAMETER (R=4)
DATA A,B/1,23E4,0.,16,0/,I/R*0/,LIST/2*'ABCD','DONE'/,
   Q/.TRUE./,C/(3.4,4.123)/
```

and the following entities are initially defined when the executable program begins execution (here, ← denotes definition):

A(1)←1.23E4,A(2)←0.,A(3)←16.,B←0
I(1)←0,I(2)←0,I(3)←0,I(4)←0
LIST(1)←'ABCD',LIST(2)←'ABCD',LIST(3)←'DONE'
Q←.TRUE.,C←(3.4,4.123)

---

*Some typical means of defining a data entity is through an assignment statement, through an input statement, and as the control variable in a DO loop or an implied DO loop.

The following operational rules apply to the use of the DATA statement:

1. The number of items in *clist* must agree with the number of entities specified in *nlist*.
2. Dummy arguments, function names, and entities in blank common must not appear in a DATA statement.
3. Names of entities in a labeled common block may only appear in a DATA statement in a BLOCK DATA program unit.

Data initialization is achieved by assigning the first value in *clist* to the first entity in *nlist*, the second value in *clist* to the second entity in *nlist*, and so forth. Thus, the type of an entity in *nlist* must agree with the corresponding value in *clist*. More specifically, if the entity in *nlist* is arithmetic, then the corresponding data value in *clist* must be arithmetic, and type conversion is performed as required. If the entity in *nlist* is logical, then the corresponding data value in *clist* must be logical. Similarly, if the entity in *nlist* is character, then the corresponding data value in *clist* must be character. Any expressions that occur in *nlist* entities, as subscripts or substring expressions, must be integer constant expressions.

The initialization of character entities requires special attention. If the length attribute of a character *nlist* entity is greater than the size of the corresponding character constant, then the character entity is padded on the right with blanks. If the length attribute of a character *nlist* entity is less than the size of the corresponding character constant, then the leftmost characters in the constant are stored and the extra characters on the right are ignored. Each character constant is used to initialize one and only one character entity.

7.5.2 Implied DO Lists

An *nlist* element may specify an implied DO list for initialization of array elements. The form of implied DO list is:

$$(dlist, i = m_1, m_2 [, m_3])$$

where *dlist* is a list of array element names and implied DO lists, and i, m_1, m_2, and m_3 specify control information as follows:

> i is an integer variable used as a control variable. (The use of a variable i does not affect its definition status in the program.)

m_1 is an initial value specified as an integer constant expression.

m_2 is a limit value specified as an integer constant expression.

m_3 is an increment value specified as an integer constant expression. (If m_3 is elided, then a default value of 1 is assumed.)

The iteration count for the implied-DO must be positive. The integer constant expression used for m_1, m_2, and m_3 may include implied DO variables of other implied-DO lists.) The following statements demonstrate DATA statements with implied DO lists:

> DATA LIMIT/1000/,(A(I),I=1,25)/25*0./
> DATA ((A(I,J),J=1,5),I=1,10)/50*1.1/
> DATA (X(I,I),I=1,100)/100*1.1/
> DATA ((A(I,J),J=1,I),I=1,3)/4*0.,25.3,4E-6/

The subject of DO loops is covered in Chapter Nine.

7.5.3 The BLOCK DATA Program Unit

The BLOCK DATA program unit* provides a means of initializing variables and arrays in labeled common. A BLOCK DATA program unit has the following structure:

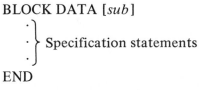

> BLOCK DATA [*sub*]
>
> Specification statements
>
> END

As shown, the BLOCK DATA program unit begins with a BLOCK DATA statement, ends with the END statement, and can only include the following specification statements: IMPLICIT, PARAMETER, DIMENSION, COMMON, SAVE, type, EQUIVALENCE, and DATA. Comment lines are also permitted. Because a BLOCK DATA program unit is processed independently** of other program units, the complete labeled common block must be declared if any variable or array element in it is initialized.

The form of the BLOCK DATA statement is:

> BLOCK DATA [*sub*]

---

*The BLOCK DATA program unit is normally referred to as the BLOCK DATA subprogram. It is felt, however, that the term "program unit" is more accurate.

**Under usual circumstances, this refers to the fact that the BLOCK DATA subprogram is compiled independently of other program units.

where *sub* is the symbolic name of the block data program unit in which the BLOCK DATA statement is included. The symbolic name *sub*, which is optional, is the external name of the program unit and it must be unique. Thus, only one BLOCK DATA program unit may have the same external name, even though an executable program may contain more than one BLOCK DATA subprogram. However, an executable program may not contain more than one unnamed BLOCK DATA program unit. The following example demonstrates the use of the BLOCK DATA concept:

```
BLOCK DATA LMDATA
REAL DISP (10,50)
INTEGER ROWS,COLS
COMMON /LMAT/ROWS,COLS,DISP
DATA ROWS,COLS/10,50/,((DISP(I,J),I=1,10),J=1,50)/500*0.01/
END
```

The following DATA statement performs the same function as the one in the BLOCK DATA program unit:

```
DATA ROWS,COLS/10,50/,DISP/500*0.0/
```

Only variables and array elements in a labeled common block may be initialized through the use of a BLOCK DATA program unit.

7.6 SPECIFICATION STATEMENTS RELATED TO SUBPROGRAMS

In general, specification statements apply equally to all types of program units. Three statements, however, relate specifically to subprograms: the EXTERNAL statement, the SAVE statement, and the INTRINSIC statement. The EXTERNAL statement is used to specify that a symbolic name represents an external procedure or a dummy procedure. The SAVE statement is used to retain the values of variables and arrays after the execution of a RETURN or END statement in a subprogram, permitting those variables or arrays to remain defined for subsequent invocations of the subprogram or for use as data in labeled common. The INTRINSIC statement is used to specify that a symbolic name identifies an intrinsic function.

7.6.1 The EXTERNAL Statement

The form of the EXTERNAL statement is:

$$\text{EXTERNAL } proc[,proc]\ldots$$

where *proc* is the symbolic name of an external procedure, a dummy procedure name, or a block data program unit.

One of the most frequent uses of the EXTERNAL statement permits an intrinsic function to be replaced by a user-written external procedure. Another use of the statement is to declare a symbolic name as an external procedure so that it can be passed to a subprogram, as in the following example:

$$\text{EXTERNAL ABFCN}$$
$$\text{CALL ANYFCN (A,M,N,ABFCN)}$$

Since the program unit in which the CALL statement is included is independent of ABFCN, it is not recognized as an external function without the EXTERNAL statement, so that a variable would be created for it. The EXTERNAL statement effectively tells the processor that ABFCN is an external procedure and that a variable should not be created.

With regard to the first application of the EXTERNAL statement, the appearance of an intrinsic function name in the statement prevents the further use of the intrinsic function in that program unit.

7.6.2 The SAVE Statement

The form of the SAVE statement is:

$$\text{SAVE } [a[,a]\ldots]$$

where each *a* is one of the following:

1. A labeled common block name preceded and followed by a slash, as in

$$\text{SAVE/LMAT/}$$

2. A variable or array name, as in

$$\text{SAVE A,B}$$

If no list is specified, then the SAVE statement is processed as though all allowable entities from that program unit were specified in the list.

The effect of the SAVE statement is to prevent named variables, arrays, and common blocks from becoming undefined after the execution of a RETURN or END statement in a subprogram. If a variable or array specified in a SAVE statement is local to a subprogram and is defined when an exit is made from the subprogram, it has the same value when the next reference is made to the subprogram.

Normally, when an exit is made from a subprogram, all variables and arrays become undefined. The only exceptions to this rule are:

1. Variable and arrays specified in a SAVE statement
2. Variables and arrays in blank common, which is effectively associated with the main program
3. Variables and arrays in a labeled common that is declared in the subprogram and in a calling program unit

Thus, all entities declared in the main program maintain their definition status throughout the processing of the entire executable program. A SAVE statement may be placed in the main program but it has no effect. Also, dummy arguments and procedure names may not appear in a SAVE statement.

The use of a SAVE statement with a labeled common block requires special attention. The case where a labeled common block is declared in the main program is covered above. In a subprogram, the specification of a labeled common block in a SAVE statement causes the values of variables and arrays in the labeled common block to retain their definition status when an exit is made from the subprogram. However, another subprogram calling that subprogram and accessing the same labeled common block without a corresponding SAVE statement will cause the variables and arrays in the labeled common block to lose their definition status when an exit is made from it. Therefore, a SAVE statement specifying a labeled common block should be included in every subprogram that accesses that common block.

A given symbolic name may appear in only one SAVE statement in a program unit.

7.6.5 The INTRINSIC Statement

The form of the INTRINSIC statement is:

INTRINSIC *fun*[,*fun*] . . .

where *fun* is the symbolic name of an intrinsic function. The specification of a symbolic name in an INTRINSIC function declares it
is an intrinsic function name. One of the most frequent uses of this
statement is to allow the name of an intrinsic function to be passed
to a subprogram, as in the following example:

```
INTRINSIC SIN
CALL DOFCN(A,M,N,SIN)
```

and the corresponding subroutine:

```
      SUBROUTINE DOFCN (ARRAY,ROWS,COLS,FCN)
      REAL ARRAY (ROWS,COLS)
      INTEGER ROWS,COLS
      DO 5 I=1,ROWS
      DO 5 J=1,COLS
    5 ARRAY (I,J)=FCN (ARRAY(I,J))
      RETURN
      END
```

The subroutine applies the function to every element in the array.
As with the EXTERNAL statement, the INTRINSIC statement prevents a variable being created for the function specified as an argument in the calling program unit.

Some obvious restrictions are in order. First, a symbolic name
may not appear in both INTRINSIC and EXTERNAL statements in
the same program unit. Second, intrinsic functions for which in-line
code is usually generated may not appear in an INTRINSIC statement. In this category are intrinsic functions for type conversion
(INT, IFIX, IDINT, FLOAT, SNGL, REAL, DBLE, CMPLX,
ICHAR, and CHAR) and intrinsic functions for selecting the largest
or smallest value (MAX, MAX0, AMAX1, AMAX0, MAX1, MIN,
MIN0, AMIN1, DMIN1, AMIN0, and MIN1). Finally, a symbolic
name of an intrinsic function may appear in only one INTRINSIC
statement in a program unit.

The appearance of an intrinsic function name in an INTRINSIC
statement does not discontinue the generic properties of that name.

8 | ASSIGNMENT STATEMENTS

8.1 OVERVIEW

The assignment statement is used to assign a value to a variable or an array element, which causes that entity to become defined. Three kinds of assignment are permitted in FORTRAN 77: arithmetic, logical, and character. Closely related is the ASSIGN statement that can be used to assign a statement number to an integer variable.

8.2 ARITHMETIC ASSIGNMENT

The arithmetic assignment statement is used to assign the value of an arithmetic expression to an arithmetic variable or array element. The form of the arithmetic assignment statement is:

$$v=e$$

where v is the symbolic name of an arithmetic variable or an element of an arithmetic array and e is an arithmetic expression evaluated at the point of reference. The type of v must be integer, real, double precision, or complex. During assignment, only the value of the entity to the left of the equals sign is replaced and references that are part of the expression retain their original values. FORTRAN 77 allows type conversion across the equals sign, as demonstrated in the

TABLE 8.1   CONVERSION RULES
FOR ARITHMETIC
ASSIGNMENT OF
THE FORM $v=e$[†][‡]

Type of v	Value Assigned
Integer	INT(e)
Real	REAL(e)
Double Precision	DBLE(e)
Complex	CMPLX(e)

[†]Depending upon the intrinsic function (FCN) used for conversion, FCN(e) may equal e, as in the case of assigning an integer value to an integer variable.
[‡]The generic functions INT, REAL, DBLE, and CMPLX are described in Appendix A.

following example:

$$I=5 \qquad (1)$$
$$J=6 \qquad (2)$$
$$A=I*J+1 \qquad (3)$$

In statements (1) and (2), 5 is assigned to I and 6 is assigned to J, respectively. In statement (3), an integer value of 31 is computed for the expression I*J+1; the value is converted to real and the real valued equivalent of 31 replaces A. The conversion rules for arithmetic assignment of the form $v=e$ is summarized in Table 8.1, which effectively requires the use of the intrinsic functions summarized in Appendix A.

8.3 LOGICAL ASSIGNMENT

The logical assignment statement is used to assign the value of a logical expression to a logical variable or array element. The form of the logical assignment statement is:

$$v=e$$

where v is the symbolic name of a logical variable or an element of a logical array and e is a logical expression evaluated at the point of reference. The following statements depict valid logical assignment statements:

LOGICAL P,Q,R,S,T

```
REAL A,B,C
INTEGER I,J,K
CHARACTER U*5,V*2
P=.TRUE.
Q=A .GT. B
R=I .NE. J .AND. Q
S=A+B .LE. C .AND. (I+J)**2+K .GT. 15 .OR. P
T=V .EQ. U(3:5)
```

In. a logical assignment statement, the value of expression *e* must be true or false.

8.4 CHARACTER STRING ASSIGNMENT

The character assignment statement is used to assign the value of a character expression to a character variable, array element, or substring. The form of the character assignment is:

$$v=e$$

where *v* is the symbolic name of a character variable, an element of a character array, or a character substring specification and *e* is a character expression evaluated at the point of reference. In the evaluation of character expression *e* and the assignment of the value of *e* to *v*, none of the character positions being replaced (i.e., defined) in *v* may be referenced in the evaluation of *e*. If the length of *e* is less than the size of *v*, then the value of *e* is padded on the right to the size of *v*. If the length of *e* is greater than the size of *v*, then the value of *e* is truncated on the right during assignment. The following examples depict character assignment:

```
CHARACTER U*5,V*3,W*7
V='ABC'
U=V//'DE'
W(4:5)=V(2:3)
```

If assignment is made to a substring, then only the character positions to which assignment is made become defined.

8.5 THE ASSIGN STATEMENT

The ASSIGN statement is used to assign a statement number to an integer variable and has the following form:

ASSIGN *s* to *i*

where *s* is the statement number of an executable statement or FORMAT statement that is used in the program unit containing the ASSIGN statement and *i* is an integer variable name. Example:

ASSIGN 5320 to IJUMP

When a statement number assignment is made, the specified integer variable may not be used as an arithmetic variable. An integer variable to which a statement number has been assigned may only be used as a statement identifier in an assigned GOTO statement or as a format identifier in an input/output statement.

An integer variable to which a statement number has been assigned may be redefined as an arithmetic integer variable and referenced accordingly.

8.6 MISCELLANEOUS COMMENTS ON ASSIGNMENT

Multiple replacement and the use of an assignment operator (i.e., =) in the body of an expression are not permitted in FORTRAN 77.

9 | CONTROL STATEMENTS

9.1 OVERVIEW

The execution of control statements affects the order in which statements are executed in a program unit. The order is normally sequential, as covered previously, and is dependent upon the order in which the various statements are included in a program unit. Control statements allow normal sequencing to be altered. This chapter covers all of the control statements, except for CALL and RETURN, which are covered with the subject of subprograms.

9.2 GOTO STATEMENTS

The GOTO statement is used to direct program control to an executable statement indicated by the statement number specified in the respective GOTO statement. Three types of GOTO statements exist in FORTRAN 77: the unconditional GOTO, the computed GOTO, and the assigned GOTO.

9.2.1 Unconditional GOTO Statement

The form of the unconditional GOTO statement is:

$$\text{GOTO } s$$

where s is the statement number of an executable statement appearing in the same program unit as the unconditional GOTO statement. Example:

$$\text{GOTO } 154$$

When the unconditional GOTO statement is executed by the processor, program control is transferred to the specified statement and normal sequential execution continues from there.

9.2.2 Computed GOTO Statement

The form of the computed GOTO statement is:

$$\text{GOTO } (s[,s]\ldots)[,]i$$

where i is an integer expression and s is the statement number of an executable statement in the same program unit as the computed GOTO statement. The statement numbers specified need not be unique. Example:

$$\text{GOTO}(100,200,200,250,9000),\text{KJMP}+1$$

The computed GOTO statement operates in the following way:

1. The integer expression, denoted above by i, is evaluated at the the point of reference.
2. Program control is transferred to the statement identifier by the ith statement number in the list following the keyword GOTO.

More specifically, in the computed GOTO statement:

$$\text{GOTO}(s_1,s_2, \ldots ,s_n),i$$

program control is passed to executable statement numbered s_i, where $1 \leqslant i \leqslant n$. If $i < 1$ or $i > n$ then program control continues with the next sequential statement following the computed GOTO statement.

9.2.3 Assigned GOTO Statement

The form of the assigned GOTO statement is:

$$\text{GOTO } i[[,](s[,s]\ldots)]$$

where i is an integer variable, defined with a statement number value, and s is the statement number of an executable statement in the same program unit as the assigned GOTO statement. Example:

$$\text{GOTO LBRNCH, (100,400,14990)}$$

When the assigned GOTO statement is executed by the processor, program control is transferred to the executable statement identified by the statement number assigned to the integer variable specified in the assigned GOTO statement and normal sequential execution continues from there. If a parenthesized list of statement numbers follows i in the above statement structure, then the statement number assigned to i must be a member of the list. The same statement number may appear more than once in the list of statement numbers.

9.3 IF STATEMENTS

The IF statements provide the conditional facility in FORTRAN 77. The arithmetic IF statement permits conditional branching. The logical IF statement permits conditional statement execution. The IF-THEN-ELSE statements permit blocks of statements to be executed on a conditional basis.

9.3.1 Arithmetic IF Statement

The form of the arithmetic IF statement is:

$$\text{IF}(e)s_1,s_2,s_3$$

where e is an arithmetic expression that can be of type integer, real, or double precision, but not complex, and s_1, s_2, and s_3 are statement numbers of executable statements in the same program unit as the arithmetic IF statement. The same statement number may be used more than once in the same arithmetic IF statement. Example:

$$\text{IF}((A+B)**2-C)100,200,300$$

The arithmetic IF statement operates in the following way:

1. The expression e is evaluated at the point of reference
2. Control is transferred to statements numbered s_1, s_2, or s_3 depending upon whether the value of e is less than, equal to, or greater than the value of zero, respectively.

After program control is transferred to one of the specified statement numbers, normal sequential execution continues from there.

9.3.2 Logical IF Statement

The form of the logical IF statement is:

$$IF(e)st$$

where e is a logical expression and st is any executable statement, excluding DO, block IF, ELSE IF, ELSE, END IF, END, or another logical IF statement. Examples:

> IF(R .LE. EPS) GO TO 4320
> IF(A .LT. 0.)A=0.0
> IF(Q) CALL MATMPY(A,M,N,B,C)

The logical IF statement operates in the following way:

1. The logical expression e is evaluated at the point of reference.
2. If the value of e is true, then st is executed. If the value of e is false, then execution continues with the next sequential statement following the logical IF statement.

The evaluation of logical expression e and the execution of st are independent in the sense that a function reference in e may affect constituents in statement st.

9.3.3 The IF-THEN-ELSE Facility

An IF-THEN-ELSE block has the following structure:

> IF(e) THEN
> [block of executable statements] *This is an IF block*
> ELSE
> [block of executable statements] *This is an ELSE block*
> END IF

where the ELSE block can be omitted, or alternately:

> IF(e) THEN
> [block of executable statements] *This is an IF block*
> ELSE IF (e) THEN

[block of executable statements]   *This is an ELSE IF block*

.

.

.

[additional ELSE IF blocks]

.

.

.

ELSE
[block of executable statements]   *This is an ELSE block*
END IF

where, again, the ELSE block can be omitted.

9.3.3.1 If Level

The proper execution of the IF-THEN-ELSE facility requires a mechanism for denoting which IF-THEN-ELSE statements correspond to each other. This mechanism is called "if level." The *if level* of a statement s has the value n_1-n_2, where n_1 is the number of block IF statements (covered next) from the beginning of the program unit up to and including s, and n_2 is the number of END IF statements in the program unit up to *but not including s*. Thus, the if level of any statement must be zero or positive, and the if level of block IF, ELSE IF, ELSE, and END IF statements must be positive. The if level of the END statement of a program unit must be zero.

9.3.3.2 Block IF Statement

The form of a block IF statement is:

IF (e) THEN

where e is a logical expression evaluated at the point of reference. A block IF statement is executed by the processor as follows:

1. The logical expression e is evaluated.
2. If the value of e is true, execution continues with the first statement in the IF block.* After the last statement in an IF block is executed, program control is transferred to the next END IF statement that has the same if level as the block IF

---

*An *IF block* is defined as the executable statements following a block IF statement up to, but not including, the next ELSE IF, ELSE, or END IF statement with the same if level as the block IF statement. An IF block may contain no statements, i.e., it may be empty.

statement. If the IF block is empty, then program control is passed directly to the next END IF statement that has the same if level as the block IF statement. If the last statement in an IF block has the effect of a transfer of control to another part of the program unit, then the control statement is executed accordingly.

3. If the value of *e* is false, execution continues with the next ELSE IF, ELSE, or END IF statement with the same if level as the block IF statement.

Program control may not be transferred into an IF block.

9.3.3.3 ELSE IF Statement

The form of an ELSE IF statement is:

$$\text{ELSE IF } (e) \text{ THEN}$$

where *e* is a logical expression evaluated at the point of reference. An ELSE IF statement is executed by the processor as follows:

1. The logical expression *e* is evaluated.
2. If the value of *e* is true, execution continues with the first statement in the ELSE IF block.* After the last statement in an ELSE IF block is executed, program control is transferred to the next END IF statement that has the same if level as the ELSE IF statement. If the ELSE IF block is empty, then program control is passed directly to the next END IF statement that has the same if level as the ELSE IF statement. If the last statement in an ELSE IF block has the effect of a transfer of control to another part of the program unit, then the control statement is executed accordingly.
3. If the value of *e* is false, execution continues with the next ELSE IF, ELSE, or END IF statement with the same if level as the ELSE IF statement.

Program control may not be transferred into an ELSE IF block.

---

*An *ELSE IF block* is defined as the executable statements following an ELSE IF statement up to, but not including, the next ELSE IF, ELSE, or END IF statement with the same if level as the ELSE IF statement. An ELSE IF block may contain no statements, i.e., it may be empty.

9.3.3.4 ELSE Statement

The form of the ELSE statement is:

ELSE

Control is passed to an ELSE block* through a false value for the logical expression in a block IF or ELSE IF statement. If program control reaches the ELSE block, then the normal sequence of execution is sequential through the END IF statement. Program control may not be transferred into an ELSE block.

9.3.3.5 END IF Statement

The form of the END IF statement is:

END IF

The END IF statement serves as a point of reference in a program unit and it performs no executable function.

An END IF statement must exist in a program unit for each block IF statement.

9.3.3.6 Notes and Example

The statement number of an ELSE IF or an ELSE statement may not be specified in an executable statement that causes program control to be transferred to those statements. This restriction does not hold for the END IF statement.

Figure 9.1 contains a flow diagram of an illustrative example. The following program segment in FORTRAN 77 is a representation of the diagram:

```
                    IF (Q) THEN
                       A=B
                       C=D
                    ELSE IF (R) THEN
                       E=F
                       G=H
                    ELSE
                       X=Y
                       Z=W
                    END IF
```

---

*An *ELSE block* is defined as the executable statements following an ELSE statement up to, but not including, the next END IF statement with the same IF level as the ELSE statement. An ELSE block may contain no statements, i.e., it may be empty.

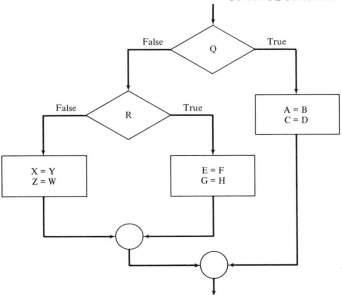

Figure 9.1   Example of IF-THEN-ELSE statements.

Block IF, ELSE IF, ELSE, and END IF can be nested, within the if level restrictions given above, to any level to satisfy the needs of a particular application.

9.4 DO STATEMENT

The DO statement is used to establish a controlled loop, specify the control variable, give the indexing parameters, and delineate the range of the loop. The controlled loop is called a *DO loop* in FORTRAN 77. The form of the DO statement is:

$$\text{DO } s \ [,] i = e_1, e_2 [, e_3]$$

where:

s is the statement number of the last statement in the range of the DO loop.

i is the symbolic name of an integer, real, or double precision variable, called the *DO variable* in FORTRAN 77.

e_1 is an integer, real, or double precision expression representing the initial value given to the DO variable.

e_2 is an integer, real, or double precision expression representing the limit value for the DO variable.

e_3 is an integer, real, or double precision expression representing the increment value for the DO variable.

The following example demonstrates a valid DO statement:

$$DO\ 500\ U=A+1,\ SQRT(B), EPS/100.$$

9.4.1 Structure of a DO Loop

The range of a DO loop consists of the sequence of executable statements following the DO statement up to and including the statement numbered s.   The following rules govern the construction of a DO loop:

1. DO loops can be nested but must not overlap.
2. If a block IF statement is in the range of a DO loop, then the corresponding END IF statement must also be in the range of the DO loop.
3. If a DO statement appears in an IF block, an ELSE IF block, or an ELSE block, then the entire DO loop (i.e., the range of the DO statement) must be contained in that block.
4. The statement numbered s in a DO loop must not be one of the following: unconditional GOTO, assigned GOTO, arithmetic IF, block IF, ELSE IF, ELSE, END IF, RETURN, STOP, END, or another DO statement.   If the statement numbered s is a logical IF statement, then it may contain any executable statement except one of the following statements in its statement body: DO, block IF, ELSE IF, ELSE, END IF, END, or another logical IF statement.

The same statement may serve as the terminal statement in two or more nested DO loops.

9.4.2 Execution of a DO Loop

The objective of a DO loop is to execute the executable statements in its range the number of times determined by the control parameters specified in the DO statement.   The process of executing a DO loop involves the following steps:

1. Executing the DO statement and activating the DO loop
2. Computing the iteration count

3. Testing the iteration count
4. Execution of the statements in the DO loop
5. Performing loop control procedures
6. Deactivation of the DO loop

Initially, a DO loop is activated when the DO statement is executed. At this time, the expressions e_1, e_2, and e_3 are evaluated, and control parameters m_1, m_2, and m_3, respectively, are determined. The expressions e_1, e_2, and e_3 are converted to the type of a DO variable in the case where the data types are not consistent. The increment m_3 may not be zero and assumes a default value of one.

The iteration count is established as the value of the following expression:

$$MAX(INT((m_2 - m_1 + m_3)/m_3), 0)$$

The increment may be positive or negative and the initial and limit values may assume appropriate values. If $m_1 > m_2$ then the iteration count is initially zero when $m_3 > 0$. Similarly, the iteration count is initially zero when $m_1 < m_2$ and $m_3 < 0$.

Loop processing begins by testing the iteration count. If it is zero, the DO loop becomes inactive and execution continues with the first executable statement following the last statement in the DO loop. If several DO loops share the terminal statement, then incrementation processing is continued.

If the iteration count is positive, the statements that comprise the DO loop are executed successively until the terminal statement is processed. This is one iteration of the loop, after which incrementation is required.

The process of *incrementation* involves the following steps:

1. The value of the DO variable is incremented by the increment value m_3.
2. The iteration count is decreased by one.
3. Execution continues with the loop processing procedure covered above.

The control parameters cannot be changed during the execution of a DO loop, since the iteration count is determined initially. The control variable can be redefined during the execution of a DO loop.

A DO loop becomes inactive when the iteration count is reduced to zero. Other ways of deactivating a DO loop are:

1. Execution of a RETURN statement in the range of the DO loop
2. Execution of a statement that transfers control outside the range of the DO loop
3. Execution of a STOP statement in the program or an abnormal program termination

Reference to a subprogram from within the range of a DO loop or in a DO statement does not deactivate a DO loop. When an exit is made from a DO loop, the DO variable retains the last value assigned to it. A DO loop may only be entered through its DO statement.

9.5 CONTINUE STATEMENT

The CONTINUE statement serves as a point of reference in a FORTRAN program and the effect of its execution is that no operational function is performed. Its form is:

CONTINUE

The CONTINUE statement is frequently used in a DO loop to provide a terminal statement, as in the following example:

```
        DO 50 I=1,N
        IF (X(I) .LT. 0.) GOTO 50
        SUM=SUM+X (I)
        PROD=PROD*X (I)
     50 CONTINUE
```

9.6 STOP AND PAUSE STATEMENTS

The form of the STOP statement is:

STOP [n]

where n is an integer constant containing five digits or less or is a character constant. When the STOP statement is executed by the processor, execution of the program is terminated and the value of n is available for an implementation-dependent purpose.

The form of the PAUSE statement is:

PAUSE [n]

where n is an integer constant containing five digits or less or is a character constant. When the PAUSE statement is executed by the processor, execution of the program ceases, but is left in a resumable state. The value n is available for an implementation-dependent purpose.   Resumption of the execution is not under control of the program. However, when execution is resumed, the execution of the PAUSE statement has no effect on the execution of the program.

9.7 END STATEMENT

The END statement denotes the physical end of a program unit. If it is executed in a main program, it has the effect of a STOP statement. If it is executed in a subprogram, it has the effect of a RETURN statement. The form of the END statement is:

END

written in columns 7 through 72 of an initial line. No other statement may begin with the letters END.

10 | INPUT AND OUTPUT CONCEPTS

10.1 SCOPE OF INPUT AND OUTPUT FACILITIES

The input and output facilities in FORTRAN 77 have been extended beyond those of the 1966 FORTRAN standard to include the capability for processing internal files and direct-access files, as well as the addition of a variety of supporting features that help make it more convenient to program input and output operations in FORTRAN and to give the programmer more direct control over the input/output system. To a large extent, the implementation of the input and output specifications in the FORTRAN 77 standard is dependent upon the processor and the host operating environment. As a result of the situation, this chapter and subsequent chapters on the FORTRAN 77 input/output system are primarily concerned with the programmer-related aspects of input and output processing.

10.2 RECORDS

The FORTRAN 77 input/output system is record oriented in the sense that each READ statement causes a record to be read and each WRITE or PRINT statement causes a record to be written or printed.

A *record* is defined to be a sequence of data values or characters, and does not necessarily correspond to a particular physical representation. In FORTRAN 77, all records are understood to be logical records, in contrast to the physical record concept. More specifically, each execution of a READ statement causes the next record to be accessed from the specified unit, which may in fact be a string of characters in storage. The amount of data that is taken from an input record is determined by the input list. Excess data is ignored. If insufficient data exists to satisfy the input list, then an error condition is generated. Each execution of a WRITE or PRINT statement causes a record to be written or printed to the specified device, which also may be an area of storage. The amount of data generated by a WRITE or PRINT statement is governed by the output list and the corresponding FORMAT statement, whenever appropriate. Records may have a length of zero. Three kinds of records exist in FORTRAN 77: formatted records, unformatted records, and endfile records.

10.2.1 Formatted Records

Formatted records are used when it is desired to read source data, display printed information in readable form, and store data in an external form, such as binary coded decimal. The data in a formatted record is edited during both the input and output processes. The length of a formatted record is measured in characters. A formatted record may only be written and read through the use of formatted input/output statements.

10.2.2 Unformatted Records

Unformatted records are used when it is desirable to store data on a storage medium and subsequently retrieve that data without having to go through an editing process. Unformatted records are stored in an internal, processor-dependent, form and may contain arithmetic, logical, or character data. The length of an unformatted record is measured in processor-dependent units, such as bits, bytes, or words, and is determined by the items in the output list. An unformatted record may only be written and read through the use of unformatted input/output statements.

10.2.3 Endfile Records

An endfile record is a means of denoting the logical end of a data file. This type of record is written by the ENDFILE statement and does not contain data. When encountered during a READ operation, an endfile record evokes an end-of-file condition.

10.3 FILES

A file is a sequence of logical records stored on an external storage medium. The characteristics of the external storage medium determine the manner in which the file can be read and written. Two types of files are defined in FORTRAN 77: external files and internal files. An internal file is actually a special case incorporated to permit movement from an area of internal (i.e., main) storage to another. Concepts that relate to files are also covered in this section. The records in a given file must be either all formatted or all unformatted.

10.3.1 External File

An external file is a set of records stored on an external storage medium, such as magnetic tape or disk storage. A file may be a deck of cards, a terminal device from which a user interacts with the processor, or a printed page. In fact, most peripheral devices may be associated with a FORTRAN 77 file. A file may be empty, which is a way of stating that it does not contain any records.

10.3.2 Internal File

An internal file is an area of internal (i.e., main) storage specified as a character variable, a character array, or a substring. Operations, such as read or write, to an internal file always involve editing so that the facility can be used to convert data from one form to another. Historically, the internal file concept is analogous to the READ TAPE zero and the READ unit zero capabilities, in FORTRAN II and FORTRAN IV, respectively, that were provided by some implementations of FORTRAN.

10.3.3 File Terminology

In communicating about files, a few terms require definition—even though the concepts are generally well known. Since a file is defined

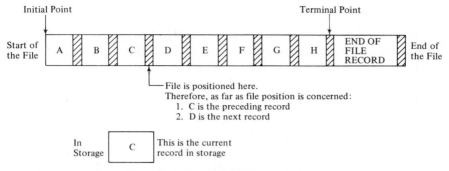

Figure 10.1   Example of file terminology.

as a sequence of records, there exists a precedence relation among records which is inherent in the example of file terminology, given in Figure 10.1, and in the following definitions:

Initial point—the file position just before the first data record.

Terminal point—the file position just following the last data record.

Current record—the existence of the record just previously read in main storage. There is no current record as far as a file is concerned since complete records are read and written.

Preceding record—the record just before the current file position. If the file is positioned at its initial point, no preceding record exists. (Alternate definition: the record just previously read or written.)

Next record—the record or record position just following the current file position. If a file is positioned at its terminal point, no next record exists. (Alternate definition: the next record to be read or written.)

A file may also have processor-dependent attributes, such as file name, blocking factors, and device allocation parameters.

10.4 ACCESS

Access refers to the order in which records are read from and written to a file. As mentioned above, access is largely dependent upon the medium employed for storage of a particular file and the manner in which the data records are organized within the file.

10.4.1 Access Attributes

Two access attributes apply to files: SEQUENTIAL and DIRECT. A given file can have either attribute or both of the attributes, depending upon the processor and operating environment. A file with the SEQUENTIAL attribute can be accessed sequentially through the use of sequential input and output statements. A file with the DIRECT attribute can be accessed directly through the use of direct access input and output statements. In all cases, however, the access attributes refer to the manner in which the FORTRAN system addresses the file and not necessarily the manner in which the underlying hardware system functions.

Files with a SEQUENTIAL attribute possess an endfile record, corresponding to the endfile condition covered below. Files with a DIRECT attribute, exclusively, do not possess an endfile record.

10.4.2 Sequential Access

Sequential access refers to a method of reading or writing a file wherein the sequence in which the records of the file are accessed can be predicted in advance. If sequential access is made to a file with the SEQUENTIAL attribute, such as a file on cards or tape, the records must be accessed in sequence—hence the name sequential access. A direct-access storage device can be used to store a file with the SEQUENTIAL attribute that is accessed sequentially. In this case, records are also read or written sequentially, with sequential input and output statements, and the underlying hardware and software system takes care of the necessary processing.

If sequential access is made to a file that also possesses the DIRECT attribute, then records are read and written by sequential order by record number.

All internal files must be accessed sequentially.

10.4.3 Direct Access

Direct access refers to a method of reading or writing a file wherein the order in which the records of the file are accessed cannot be predicted in advance. Direct access applies to files that can be read or written in any order and the implied order of the records is their record number and not the order in which the records are written.

The *record number* is an integer value that is specified when a record to a DIRECT file is written. All records of a DIRECT file must have the same length, and must not be synthesized using list-directed editing.

10.4.4 Access to Internal Files

An internal file is always positioned at its initial point and must be accessed sequentially. Thus, an internal file contains only one logical record.

10.5 UNITS

In FORTRAN 77, a data file is referred to as a unit. For an external file, a unit is specified as an integer value, which must be zero or positive. For an internal file, a unit is specified as a character variable, character array, character array element, or character substring.

10.5.1 Connection

The association of a unit with a data file is referred to as *connection*. A unit can be implicitly connected by the processor or explicitly connected by an OPEN statement.

All units in FORTRAN 77 are preconnected. The OPEN statement is used to specify or change control information for a unit, connect a unit after it has been disconnected, or to change the data file to which a unit is connected. A unit may be connected to only one data file at any given time. However, a specific unit designator may be disconnected from one data file and then connected to another data file.

10.5.2 Disconnection

A unit is disconnected from a data file when one of the following occurs:

1. A CLOSE statement specifying that particular unit is executed.
2. An OPEN statement specifying the same unit but another data file is executed. (This is a processor dependent function.)
3. Execution of the program is terminated.

Input and output statements, other than OPEN, CLOSE, and IN-QUIRE, must not reference disconnected units.

10.6 CONTROL INFORMATION LIST

A control information list is used in a READ, WRITE, or PRINT statement to specify the following control information about an input or an output operation:

1. Unit
2. Format
3. Record number
4. Input/output status
5. Error return
6. End-of-file return

Collectively, the six specifiers are known as the "control information list," or alternatively, the *cilist*.

10.6.1 Syntax of the List

A *cilist* is a list comprised of the following positional and keyword parameters:

$$[UNIT=]u$$
$$[FMT=]f$$
$$REC = rn$$
$$IOSTAT = ios$$
$$ERR = s$$
$$END = s$$

The unit and format specifiers must be placed in positions one and two, respectively, of the list if they are used as positional parameters. Otherwise, the items in *cilist* may be written in any order. Examples:

READ(5,9000,END=1000)A,B,C,D
WRITE(99,8000,REC=ISEQ,ERR=1500)CARRAY
READ(FMT=9000,END=1000,UNIT=5)A,B,C,D

If the format specifier is present, then a formatted input or output operation is denoted; otherwise, an unformatted input or output operation is denoted. If the record specifier is present, then a direct access input or output operation is denoted; otherwise, a sequential input or output operation is denoted.

10.6.2 Unit Specifier

The unit specifier takes the form:

$$[UNIT=]\,u$$

where u is one of the following:

1. An integer expression, which must have a zero or positive value, specifying an external unit identifier
2. An asterisk specifying a system unit that is preconnected for sequential input or sequential output to an external unit
3. An internal file identifier that takes the form of a symbolic name of a character variable, character array, character array element, or character substring

A given unit specifier has the same meaning in all program units of an executable program.

10.6.3 Format Specifier

A format specifier takes the form:

$$[FMT=]\,f$$

where f is one of the following:

1. The statement number of a FORMAT statement in the same program unit as the format specifier
2. An integer variable that has been ASSIGNed the statement number of a FORMAT statement in the same program unit as the format specifier
3. A character array name
4. A character expression, with the exception of one containing a dummy argument with a length specified with an asterisk
5. An asterisk denoting list directed editing

If the keyword is omitted from the format specifier, then it must also be omitted from the unit specifier.

10.6.4 Record Specifier

The record specifier takes the form:

$$REC = rn$$

where *rn* is an integer expression which has a positive value computed at the point of reference. The record specifier denotes the number of the record to be read or written in a direct access input/output operation.

10.6.5 Input/Output Status Specifier

An input/output status specifier takes the form:

$$IOSTAT = ios$$

where *ios* is an integer variable or element of an integer array. Upon completion of the corresponding input or output statement, *ios* is defined as one of the following:

1. *ios* contains a zero value denoting a successful operation—i.e., no error and no end-of-file.
2. *ios* contains an implementation-defined positive integer value if an error condition occurred.
3. *ios* contains an implementation-defined negative integer value if an end of file condition occurred without an error condition.

The appropriate value is assigned to *ios* regardless of whether the end of file or error specifiers is additionally present in the *cilist*.

10.6.6 Error Specifier

An error specifier takes the form:

$$ERR = s$$

where *s* is the statement number of an executable statement in the same program unit as the error specifier. If an error condition is encountered during the execution of an input or output statement containing the error specifier, then program control is transferred to the specified statement number upon termination of the input or output operation and the input or output statement. As mentioned above, the input/output status specifier is defined accordingly.

10.6.7 End-of-File Specifier

An end-of-file specifier takes the form:

$$END = s$$

where s is the statement number of an executable statement in the same program unit as the end-of-file specifier. If an end-of-file condition is encountered during the execution of a READ statement containing the end-of-file specifier and no associated error condition occurs, then program control is transferred to the specified statement number and the read operation is terminated. As mentioned above, the input/output status specifier is defined accordingly.

10.7 INPUT/OUTPUT LIST

An input/output list is used in a READ, WRITE, or PRINT statement to specify the data that participates in a data transfer operation. An input/output list is a simple list, a simple list enclosed in parentheses, an implied-DO list, or two input/output lists separated by a comma. Each of these concepts is described below.

10.7.1 Simple List

A simple list is a series of data specifications, separated by commas. Input and output lists differ slightly because an expression may be included as a list element in an output list but may not be used in an input list.

10.7.1.1 Input List

A simple input list is one of the following:

1. A variable
2. An array
3. A character substring
4. An element of an array

Examples:

```
READ(5,9000,END=5000)A,B(I,J+1),C(4:6)
READ(KFILE,REC=IREC,ERR=6000)N,RLIST(N,3),CTABLE
```

10.7.1.2 Output List

A simple output list is one of the following:

1. A variable
2. An array
3. A character substring
4. An element of an array
5. An expression, with the exception of a character expression containing a dummy argument with a length attribute specified with an asterisk

Examples:

WRITE(6,8000,ERR=50)'PAGE NO',N,SQRT(R)+1.23,A(I,J/K+1)
WRITE(LTR,REC=KREC,ERR=7000)CLIST,M,RTABLE(M/2-1)

10.7.2 Implied-DO List

The form of an implied-DO list is:

$$(dlist, i = e_1, e_2 [,e_3])$$

where *dlist* is an input/output list, i is the control variable, and e_1, e_2, and e_3 are control parameters. The values and operational conventions governing i, e_1, e_2, and e_3 are exactly the same as for the DO statement. The rules that apply to the execution of a DO loop apply equally to the data transfer specified in an implied-DO list. The control variable i may not appear as an input or output variable in *dlist*; however, *dlist* may include other implied-DO lists.* During input, the expressions e_1, e_2, and e_3 may not contain entities specified in *dlist*, but may contain entities in a prior portion of an input list:

Examples:

READ(3,9500,END=2000)N,M,((A(I,J),J=1,M),I=1,N)
WRITE(17,REC=KREC,ERR=3000)(B(K+1),K=LIM/2+1,I),TOP

When an inplied-DO list appears in an input/output list, the entities specified in *dlist* participate in a data transfer for each iteration of the implied-DO list, wherein the control variable i assumes values specified in the implied-DO control parameters.

*The control variable i may be used in a subscript in *dlist*.

10.7.3 Arrays

If an array name is used in an input/output list, the elements in the array participate in a data transfer as though each element were explicitly specified in the input/output list in column order. Thus, the statements:

REAL A(2,3)

. . .

READ(*,100)A

is exactly equivalent to:

REAL A(2,3)

. . .

READ(*,100)A(1,1)A(2,1),A(1,2),A(2,2),A(1,3),A(2,3)

10.8 DATA TRANSFER OPERATIONS

During an input or an output operation, data are transferred between data records and input/output list elements. Each list item is processed completely before the next item is processed and the order of processing is the same as the order of items in the input/output list. Thus, an entity defined in an input statement may be used in the definition of an entity appearing later in the list, as in:

READ(KFILE)N, (A(I),I=1,N)

OR

READ(IFILE,5000)N,(A(I),I=1,N)

Three restrictions exist:

1. An entity in an input list may not coincide with the format specified in the same statement.
2. All entities specified in an output statement must be defined prior to the execution of the output statement.
3. An entity in an input list for an internal file operation must not coincide with the storage occupied by the internal file.

The following sections describe various operational conventions as they apply to either unformatted or formatted data transfer operations.

10.8.1 Unformatted Data Transfer Operations

During the execution of an unformatted input or output statement, one record is either read or written. In the execution of an unformatted input statement, the record must contain at least as many values as the number of values specified in the input list, and the data type of values from the input record must agree with the entities defined through the input statement. Character values from an input record must have the same length attributes as the character entities they are used to define. Excess values are ignored and an insufficient number of values engenders an error condition.

In the execution of an unformatted output statement, the following conventions exist:

1. For sequential access, the size of the output record is determined by the output list.
2. For direct access, the output list may not specify more values that can be placed in the output record. An output record that is not completely filled is left partially defined.

Unformatted data transfer statements can only be specified for external data files.

10.8.2 Formatted Data Transfer Operations

During a formatted input or output operation, data values are edited under format control just prior to storage or retrieval, respectively. During an input operation, a data record is read prior to the editing operation. Thus, each execution of a READ statement causes at least one record to be read. The amount of data to be taken from the record is determined by the input list. The position and form of that data is governed by the corresponding FORMAT statement. Excess data is ignored, and insufficient data causes an error condition. The FORMAT statement may cause additional records to be read. In the case of direct access, the record number is increased by one prior to each succeeding read operation.

Each execution of a WRITE statement causes at least one record to be written to the specified unit. The amount of data that is written is determined collectively by the output list and the format specification. A data value is retrieved from storage, converted to an external form through the use of a field descriptor, and placed in the output record. When the output list is satisfied, the output record is complete, regardless of whether unused field descriptors exist in the format specification. The record is then written or moved to the specified unit. The FORMAT statement may cause additional records to be written. In the case of direct access, blank characters are used to fill a record when the characters specified by the output list and the format specification do not fill the output record. Output editing for direct access may not generate more characters than can fit into an output record. When an additional record must be written under format control with direct access, the record number is increased by one just prior to the write operation.

10.8.3 Print Files

The first character of each output record in a print file controls vertical spacing. This character is known as the "carriage control character." The remaining characters in a record are printed starting with the left hand margin. The following interpretation of the carriage control character is established:

Character	Vertical Spacing Before Printing
Blank	One line
0 (zero)	Two lines
1	To first line of next page
+	No advance (overprint of last line)

Records that contain no characters, generated by slash editing in a FORMAT statement, cause a blank line to be printed. (This is accomplished through one line vertical spacing and the printing of a blank line.)

10.8.4 List Directed Input and Output

An asterisk used to specify the format identifier in an input or an output statement denotes a list directed operation. List directed operations involve input and output editing but do not utilize a format specification. Input and output data are separated in a data record by commas or blank characters, as determined by a particular implementation of FORTRAN 77. This subject is covered in later chapters along with other format specifications.

10.8.5 File Position

After an end-of-file condition during an input operation or the execution of an ENDFILE statement during an output operation, a sequential file is positioned after the endfile record. In this case, additional data transfer operations may not be performed without repositioning. A file may be repositioned through the use of REWIND or BACKSPACE statements.

11 | INPUT AND OUTPUT STATEMENTS

11.1 OVERVIEW

The input and output statements in FORTRAN 77 are grouped into three classes: data transfer statements, auxiliary statements, and file positioning statements. The set of data transfer statements contains the READ, WRITE, and PRINT statements. The set of auxiliary statements contains the OPEN, CLOSE, and INQUIRE statements. The set of file positioning statements contains the BACKSPACE, ENDFILE, and REWIND statements. A complete understanding of the information contained in this chapter requires a familiarity with the "input/output concepts" given in the preceding chapter.

11.2 DATA TRANSFER STATEMENTS

Data transfer statements are used to transfer information between internal storage and an external device or between two areas of internal storage. The two forms of the READ statement perform an input function; the WRITE and PRINT statements perform output functions.

11.2.1 READ Statement

The READ statement takes the following form:

READ(*cilist*) [*iolist*]

where *cilist* is a control information list and *iolist* is an optional input list; both types of lists were covered previously. This form of the READ statement can be used for both formatted and unformatted input from the device specified in the *cilist*.

An alternate form of the READ statement is:

READ *f* [,*iolist*]

where *f* is a format identifier and *iolist* is an optional input list. This form of the READ statement can be used for formatted input from the system input device.

Examples:

```
READ (2,1500,END=5000)A,B,C,D
READ (12,REC=LRT,ERR=8000) (CAB(I,J),J=1,N)
READ 50,X,Y,Z,W
```

11.2.2 WRITE Statement

The WRITE statement takes the following form:

WRITE (*cilist*) [*iolist*]

where *cilist* is a control information list and *iolist* is an optional output list; both types of lists were covered previously. The WRITE statement can be used for both formatted and unformatted output to the device specified in the *cilist*.

Examples:

```
WRITE(*,8500)A,B,NLOC, (TOM(I),I=1,NLOC)
WRITE(1)BIGLST
```

11.2.3 PRINT Statement

The PRINT statement takes the following form:

PRINT *f* [,*iolist*]

where *f* is a format identifier and *iolist* is an optional output list. The PRINT statement can be used for formatted output to the system output device.

Examples:

        PRINT 10, (LIST (K) ,K=1,N+1)
        PRINT *,P1,P2,P3
        PRINT *, 'AREA IS',A, 'LENGTH IS', L

11.3 AUXILIARY STATEMENTS

Auxiliary statements can be used to explicitly open or close a file or inquire about the status of a file or unit.

11.3.1 OPEN Statement

The OPEN statement can be used to connect a file to a unit and has the following form:

OPEN(*olist*)

where *olist* is the list of the following specifiers:

        [UNIT =]u
        IOSTAT = *ios*
        ERR = *s*
        FILE = *fin*
        STATUS = *sta*
        ACCESS = *acc*
        FORM = *fm*
        RECL = *rl*
        BLANK = *blnk*

The UNIT specifier is required and identifies the number of an external unit.   The other specifiers are optional but must not appear more than once in a single OPEN statement. The other specifiers are described below.

The *input/output status specifier* (IOSTAT) specifies the variable to be defined where a file is connected with the OPEN statement. A zero value for *ios* denotes a "no error" condition.   A positive implementation-dependent value for *ios* denotes an error condition. Example:

IOSTAT = IOVAL

The *error specifier* (ERR) specifies a statement number to which program control should be transferred when an error condition arises during the execution of an OPEN statement. Example:

ERR = 5000

The *file specifier* (FILE) is a character expression giving the name of the external file to be connected. The name must be recognized by the processor. Example:

FILE = 'AFILE'

The *status specifier* (STATUS) is a character expression, which when trailing blanks are removed, specifies one of the following:

OLD

NEW

SCRATCH

UNKNOWN

The OLD, NEW, and SCRATCH options correspond to appropriate file specifications; the meaning of the UNKNOWN specifier is implementation dependent. Example:

STATUS = 'NEW'

The *access specifier* (ACCESS) is a character expression, which when trailing blanks are removed, specifies one of the following:

DIRECT

SEQUENTIAL

The default value is SEQUENTIAL. Example:

ACCESS = 'DIRECT'

The *form specifier* (FORM) is a character expression, which when trailing blanks are removed, specifies one of the following:

FORMATTED

UNFORMATTED

The default value for sequential access is FORMATTED and the default value for direct access is UNFORMATTED. Example:

FORM = 'UNFORMATTED'

The *record length specifier* (RECL) is a positive integer expression, denoting the length in characters or processor-dependent units for formatted and unformatted files, respectively. This specifier is required for direct access files and is ignored for sequential access files. Example:

$$RECL = LENREC$$

The *blank specifier* (BLANK) is a character expression, which when trailing blanks are removed, specifies one of the following:

NULL
ZERO

The default value is NULL. The NULL specifier indicates that blank characters in a numeric input field is to be ignored. The ZERO specifier indicates that blank characters in a numeric input field, except for leading blanks, is to be interpreted as zeros. Example:

$$BLANK = 'ZERO'$$

An OPEN statement to an already connected unit may be executed. If the files are not the same, then the old file is closed and the new one is opened. If the files are the same, then all specifiers, with the exception of the BLANK option, must be the same.

11.3.2 CLOSE Statement

The CLOSE statement can be used to disconnect a file from a unit and has the following form:

$$CLOSE \ (cllist)$$

where *cllist* is a list of the following specifiers:

[UNIT =]u
IOSTAT = ios
ERR = s
STATUS = sta

The UNIT specifier is required and identifies the number of an external unit. The other specifiers are optional but must not appear more than once in a single CLOSE statement. The other specifiers are described below.

The *input/output status specifier* (IOSTAT) specifies the variable to be defined when a file is disconnected with the CLOSE statement.

A zero value for *ios* denotes a "no error" condition. A positive implementation-dependent value for *ios* denotes an error condition. Example:

$$IOSTAT = K$$

The *error specifier* (ERR) specifies a statement number to which program control should be transferred when an error condition arises during the execution of the CLOSE statement. Example:

$$ERR = 6000$$

The *status specifier* (STATUS) is a character expression, which when trailing blanks are removed, specifies one of the following:

KEEP
DELETE

The KEEP and DELETE options correspond to appropriately named file dispositions. If a file has been opened for SCRATCH, then KEEP must not be specified in the CLOSE statement. The default value is DELETE for SCRATCH files and KEEP otherwise. Example:

STATUS = 'DELETE'

A CLOSE statement need not be executed from the same program unit in which a file was opened.

11.3.3 INQUIRE Statement

The INQUIRE statement can be used to determine the current status of a file attribute and has the following form:

INQUIRE (*ilist*)

where *ilist* is a list of specifiers for the INQUIRE statement. Two forms of the INQUIRE statement are permitted: inquiry by file and inquiry by unit. When an inquiry by file is made, the file name but not the unit name is specified. When an inquiry by unit is made, the unit number but not the file name is specified. In either case, the processor supplies information as specified in the list of specifiers. Each of the following specifiers may be included in single INQUIRE statement at most one time:

$$IOSTAT = ios$$
$$ERR = s$$

$$EXIST = ex$$
$$OPENED = od$$
$$NUMBER = num$$
$$NAMED = nmd$$
$$NAME = fn$$
$$ACCESS = acc$$
$$SEQUENTIAL = seq$$
$$DIRECT = dir$$
$$FORM = fm$$
$$FORMATTED = fmt$$
$$UNFORMATTED = unf$$
$$RECL = rcl$$
$$NEXTREC = nr$$
$$BLANK = blnk$$

The specifiers are described in Table 11.1.

11.4 FILE POSITIONING STATEMENTS

File positioning statements are defined for files with sequential access. Each of the file positioning statements uses the following parameters:

1. u is an external input/output unit identifier
2. *alist* is a list of the following specifiers:

$$[UNIT =]u$$
$$IOSTAT = ios$$
$$ERR = s$$

where each of the constituents has been defined previously in this chapter The unit specifier (u) must be included in *alist* and the other specifiers may be included at most one time in a single file positioning statement.

File positioning statements apply only to external files.

11.4.1 BACKSPACE Statement

The BACKSPACE statement can be used to position a data file before the previous record and has the following forms:

$$BACKSPACE\ u$$
$$BACKSPACE\ (alist)$$

TABLE 11.1   TABLE OF SPECIFIERS AND THEIR MEANING FOR THE INQUIRE STATEMENT

Specifier	Data Type	Meaning
FILE = *fin*	Character expression	Specifies file name for inquiry by file name.
UNIT = *u*	Integer expression with a positive value	Specifies unit number for inquiry by unit.
IOSTAT = *ios*	Integer variable or array element	*ios* =0 if no error; *ios* = positive value if error condition exists.
ERR = *s*	Statement number	Control is transferred to specified executable statement if error condition on named file or unit exists.
EXIST = *ex*	Logical variable or array element	*ex* = .TRUE. if named file exists; *ex* = .FALSE. otherwise.
OPENED = *od*	Logical variable or array element	*od* = .TRUE. if named file or unit has been opened; *od* = .FALSE. otherwise.
NUMBER = *num*	Integer variable or array element	*num* is the unit number of the external named file; if no unit is connected to the named file, *num* is undefined.
NAMED = *nmd*	Logical variable or array element	*nmd* = .TRUE. if specified unit has a name; *nmd* = .FALSE. otherwise.
NAME = *fn*	Character variable or array element	*fn* is the external name of the specified unit; if the file has no name or is not connected, *fn* is undefined.
ACCESS = *acc*	Character variable or array element	*acc* contains SEQUENTIAL or DIRECT depending upon whether specified unit or file was connected for sequential or unit access, respectively. If the file is not connected, *acc* is undefined.
SEQUENTIAL = *seq*	Character variable or array element	*seq* contains YES if connected for sequential access. NO if not connected for sequential access, and UNKNOWN if the processor is unable to determine the access type.

DIRECT = *dir*	Character variable or array element	*dir* contains YES if connected for direct access, NO if not connected for direct access, and UNKNOWN if the processor is not able to determine the access type.
FORM = *fm*	Character variable or array element	*fm* contains FORMATTED if connected for formatted data transfer, UNFORMATTED if connected for unformatted data transfer, and is not defined if the file is undefined.
FORMATTED = *fmt*	Character variable or array element	*fmt* contains YES if connected for formatted data transfer, No if not connected for formatted data transfer, and UNKNOWN if the processor is unable to determine the form of data transfer.
UNFORMATTED=*unf*	Character variable or array element	*unf* contains YES if connected for unformatted data transfer, NO if not connected for unformatted data transfer, and UNKNOWN if the processor is unable to determine the form of data transfer.
RECL = *rcl*	Integer variable or array element	*rcl* contains the record length of the specified unit or file connected for direct access, measured in characters for formatted records and processor-dependent units for unformatted records. If the file is not connected for direct access, *rcl* is undefined.
NEXTREC = *nr*	Integer variable or array element	*nr* is assigned the *next* record number to be read or written for direct access on the specified unit or file. If no records have been read or written, *nr* = 1. If the file is not connected, not connected for direct access, or its status is indeterminate, *nr* is undefined.
BLANK = *blnk*	Character variable or array element	*blnk* contains ZERO or NULL, depending upon the blank control in effect. If the specified file is not connected or not connected for formatted data transfer, *blnk* is undefined.

If there is no preceding record, the file position is not changed. If the preceding record is an endfile record, then the BACKSPACE statement positions the file before the endfile record. The BACK-SPACE statement may not be used for files that have been written using list directed output. Examples:

BACKSPACE N
BACKSPACE (UNIT=6, IOSTAT=KZ, ERR=5500)

11.4.2 ENDFILE Statement

The ENDFILE statement can be used to write an endfile record and has the following forms:

ENDFILE u
ENDFILE $(alist)$

After an endfile record has been written, the specified file is positioned after the endfile record. An endfile record may be written to a file that is connected but to which no data records have been written. Examples:

ENDFILE KFILE
ENDFILE (12,ERR=8200)

11.4.3 REWIND Statement

The REWIND statement can be used to position a file at its initial point and has the following forms:

REWIND u
REWIND $(alist)$

If the specified file is already at its initial point, the file position is not changed. Example:

REWIND 10
REWIND (NFILE,IOSTAT=NVAL)

The BACKSPACE, ENDFILE, and REWIND statements may be used with unformatted as well as formatted data files.

12 | FORMAT SPECIFICATION

12.1 OVERVIEW

A format specification is used with formatted input and output statements to permit conversion and data editing under program control. The format specification provides information to the processor on the structure of a formatted data record. During input, field descriptors are used to describe the various external data fields and a correspondence is established between a data field and an input list element. During output, field descriptors specify how internal data is to be recorded in character form on the external medium and a correspondence is established between an output list element and an external data field.

The use of a format specification to control formatted input or output is an explicit means of doing input and output editing. When an asterisk is used in place of a format identifier, list-directed formatting is specified. This topic is covered as a separate section in this chapter.

12.2 ESTABLISHING A FORMAT SPECIFICATION

A format specification may be established through the use of a FORMAT statement or through the use of a character entity defined with a set of character values that take the form of a format specification.

12.2.1 FORMAT Statement

The FORMAT statement can be used to establish a format specification and takes the following form:

$$\text{FORMAT } fs$$

where fs is a format specification, as described below. The FORMAT statement must have a statement number so that it can be referenced in an input or an output statement. The FORMAT statement is the only statement in FORTRAN 77 wherein a statement number is required. Example:

$$9000 \text{ FORMAT}(10X,I5,3F12.6/(1X,I2,10I4))$$

the FORMAT statement is a nonexecutable statement.

12.2.2 Format Stored as a Character Entity

In a formatted input or output statement, one of the options for the format identifier is that it can be a character array name, a character variable, a character array element, or a character expression. The characters comprising the character entity must have the same form as a format specification. Thus, a character format specification may be read in during program execution or it can be synthesized as a character expression.

A character format specification must begin with a left parenthesis, end with a right parenthesis, and be comprised of contiguous character storage units in which field descriptors, field separators, and other edit control descriptors are contained.

12.2.3 Form of a Format Specification

The form of a format specification is given as:

$$([q_1 t_1 z_1 t_2 z_2 \cdots t_n z_n q_2])$$

where:

1. Each q_i is one or more slashes, a colon, or is empty.
2. Each t_i is a field descriptor, an edit control descriptor, or a series of field descriptors or edit control descriptors.

3. Each z_i is a field separator (comma, slash, colon, series of slashes, or parentheses.)

The field and edit control descriptors are summarized in Table 12.1.

12.2.4 Editing

Editing is performed through the joint interaction of an item from an input/output list and a field descriptor. If the input/output list contains at least one item, then the format specification must contain at least one field descriptor. An empty format specification can be used only if the corresponding input/output list is also empty. In this situation, one record is skipped for input and a record with no characters is written for output.

Unless denoted otherwise, format specifications are interpreted from left to right, and input and output records are edited from left to right. A repetition factor indicates a list of the specified field descriptors. If the format specification is exhausted but there are remaining items in the input/output list, format control is returned to the last open parenthesis. In this case, a new record is read or the current record is written. (In the case of direct access, the record number is increased by one.)

The storage area for output record editing is always initialized to blank characters.

12.3 FIELD AND EDIT CONTROL DESCRIPTORS

Each of the field and edit control descriptors, summarized in Table 12.1, is described in this section. An elementary knowledge of FORTRAN concepts is needed for full comprehension of the subject matter.

12.3.1 Numeric Editing

The I,F,E,D, and G field descriptors are used for numeric editing. Unless specified otherwise or controlled by other edit control descriptors, the following rules apply:

1. Leading blanks are not significant for input. For output, leading zeros are suppressed. A plus sign is not printed; however, a minus sign if applicable is printed.

TABLE 12.1   FIELD AND EDIT CONTROL DESCRIPTORS

Code	Meaning in FORTRAN 77
$a\mathrm{I}w$	Describes integer data fields
$a\mathrm{I}w.m$	Describes integer data fields
$pa\mathrm{F}w.d$	Describes real data fields
$pa\mathrm{E}w.d$	Describes real data fields
$pa\mathrm{E}w.d\mathrm{E}e$	Describes real data fields
$pa\mathrm{D}w.d$	Describes double precision data fields
$pa\mathrm{G}w.d$	Describes integer or real data fields
$pa\mathrm{G}w.d\mathrm{E}e$	Describes integer or real data fields
$a\mathrm{L}w$	Describes logical data fields
$a\mathrm{A}$	Describes character data fields
$a\mathrm{A}w$	Describes character data fields
'$h_1 h_2 \ldots h_w$'	Describes character data fields
$w\mathrm{H}h_1 h_2 \ldots h_w$	Describes Hollerith data fields
Tc	Moves the current position pointer to the specified character position in an external data record
TLs	Moves the current position backward the specified number of character positions
TRs	Moves the current position pointer forward the specified number of character positions
wX	Indicates that a field is to be skipped on input or filled with blanks on output
/	Indicates that next record should be read, or the current record should be written
:	Indicates an output operation should be terminated if no output list items remain
S	Indicates that normal sign control should be resumed
SP	Indicates a plus sign should be inserted
SS	Indicates that a plus sign should not be inserted
kP	Denotes a scale factor
BN	Indicates that blank characters should be ignored
BZ	Indicates that blank characters should be treated as zeros
$a(\ldots)$	Denotes a group format specification

Where: a is an optional repeat count. If a is omitted, the code or group of codes is used once.

w is an unsigned nonzero integer constant specifying the width of a data field.

m is an unsigned integer constant that indicates the number of digits that must be displayed in an integer output field.

d is an unsigned integer constant specifying the number of places to the right of the decimal point.

e is an unsigned nonzero integer constant specifying the number of digits in an exponent field.

TABLE 12.1 (*Continued*)

Code	Meaning in FORTRAN 77
	p is an optional scale factor designator of the form *k*P. *k* is a negative or unsigned integer constant. *c* is an unsigned nonzero integer constant denoting a position in a record. *s* is an unsigned integer denoting a displacement in a record. . . . is a group format specification. Field and edit control descriptors or additional group format specifications are within the parentheses.

2. For input with F,E,D, and G descriptors, the decimal point in the input field overrides the *d* specification.
3. For output, fields are right justified. If the field width is insufficient, asterisks are produced.

Numeric field descriptors must be separated by field separators, such as the comma (,), slash (/), or colon (:).

12.3.1.1 I Editing

The *I field descriptor* is used for conversion between an internal integer data item and an external integer in decimal form. The form of an I format specification is:

$$I_w$$

where *w* is the size of the external field, including blanks and a sign. On output, the sign is printed only if the number is negative. A decimal point is not permitted in an input field. For example, on input, the external values ƀƀ12,ƀ621ƀ, and −ƀ210ƀ using format specifications I4, I5, and I6, respectively, cause the values 12, 6210, and −2100 to be stored. For output, the values −987 and 123 using format specifications I5 and I4, respectively, cause the following fields:

$$ƀ{-}987 \text{ and } ƀ123$$

to be generated. For all numeric input conversions, leading blanks are ignored and all trailing blanks are treated as zeros. An all-blank field is regarded as zero. For all output conversions, the output field is right justified. Leading blanks are supplied, as required.

A variation to the I field descriptor takes the following form:

$$I_w.m$$

For input, the I$w.m$ field descriptor is treated identically to that of the Iw field descriptor. For output, the I$w.m$ is treated identically to the Iw descriptor, except that m digits are to be displaced—including leading zeros if any. If the output value is zero and m is also zero, a blank output field is displayed.

12.3.1.2 F Editing

The *F field descriptor* is used for conversion between an internal real data item and an external real number in decimal form without an exponent. The form of an F field descriptor is:

$$F w.d$$

where w is the width of the field, including blanks, the sign, and the decimal point and d is the number of places to the right of the decimal point. On *input*, use of the decimal point is optional. If the decimal point is not used on input, then the rightmost d digits in the field are interpreted as decimal places. If the decimal point is used with input data, then it overrides d. On *output*, the decimal point is always generated with d decimal places to the right of it. Thus, with F field descriptor F6.2, the following input values achieve the same result (where ♭ denotes the blank character):

$$♭♭-123 \quad ♭-1.23 \quad -1.230 \quad -1.23♭$$

and cause the value $-.123 \times 10^1$ to be placed in main storage. On output, for example, the values $.98134 \times 10^2$ and $-.63472 \times 10^1$ are converted using field descriptors F7.2 and F8.3, respectively, so that the values

$$♭♭98.13 \text{ and } ♭♭-6.347$$

are generated.

The input field for F editing may optionally be followed by a base 10 exponent that takes one of the following forms:

1. A signed integer constant, so that an example of a valid data field would be .523-4 meaning $.523 \times 10^{-4}$.
2. The letter E followed by optional blanks followed by an optionally signed integer constant, so that an example of a valid data field would be .523E-4 meaning $.523 \times 10^{-4}$.
3. The letter D followed by optional blanks followed by an op-

tionally signed integer constant, so that an example of a valid data field would be .523D− 4 meaning .523×10⁻⁴.

An input value may specify more precision than is maintained by the processor.

12.3.1.3 E Editing

The *E field descriptor* is designed for use with real data represented in exponential notation on the external medium.   The form of an E field descriptor is:

$$Ew.d$$

where *w* is the width of the field and *d* is the number of decimal places.   For *input*, the use of an actual decimal point overrides *d*, as with the F field descriptor.   The exponent takes the form: E±*ee*, where the sign may be omitted if the exponent is positive and leading zeros in the exponent need not be written.   If the exponent is signed, then the letter E may be omitted.   The width indicator *w* must include the exponent.   The exponent should be right justified in the field since blank characters are interpreted as zeros.   Using an input E field descriptor of E12.5, all of the following fields cause the same real value of .314159×10¹ to be stored:

$$3.14159E0$$
$$314.159E− 2$$
$$314159E0$$
$$.314159+1$$

For output, the E field descriptor produces a decimal number of the form:

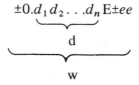

where plus signs are replaced with blank characters during output editing.   Thus the statements:

$$A=987.123$$
$$WRITE(6,9000)A$$
$$9000 \quad FORMAT(1H ,E15.7)$$

would cause the following value to be printed:

$$\not b\not b0.9871230E\ 03$$

where the $\not b$ denotes a blank character. As with input, the magnitude of w must include space for the exponent.

As with F editing, the exponent part of an input value may be optionally omitted, and an input value may specify more precision than is maintained by the processor.

A variation to the E field descriptor takes the following form:

$$Ew.dEe$$

For input, the Ew.dEe field descriptor is treated identically to that of the Ew.d field descriptor. For output, Ew.dEe is treated identically to the Ew.d descriptor, except that an exponent field of e digits is to be displayed.

12.3.1.4 D Editing

The *D field descriptor* is used for the editing and conversion of double precision data. The D field descriptor takes the form:

$$Dw.d$$

and operates in precisely the same fashion as the E field descriptor, except that the exponent is expressed with a D instead of an E.

12.3.1.5 Complex Editing

A *complex data item,* which is composed of two real components, is edited using two consecutive real field descriptors. For example, the statements:

```
        COMPLEX ARC
        ARC= (4.0,3.0)
        WRITE(6,9001)ARC
9001    FORMAT(1H ,2F5.1)
```

would cause the following values to be printed:

$$\not b\not b4.0\not b\not b3.0$$

Complex input operates in analogous fashion.

12.3.1.6 G Editing

A *general (G) field descriptor* is defined for the conversion and editing of real data where the magnitude of the data is not known beforehand. The form of the G field descriptor is:

$$Gw.d$$

For input, the G field descriptor is equivalent to an F field descriptor. For output, the G field descriptor is equivalent to the following:

Magnitude of Real *Data Item*	*Equivalent Conversion* *Performed*
$0.1 \leqslant v < 1$	$F(w-4).d,4X$
$1 \leqslant v < 10$	$F(w-4).(d-1),4X$
$10 \leqslant v < 100$	$F(w-4).(d-2),4X$
.	.
.	.
.	.
$10^{d-2} \leqslant v < 10^{d-1}$	$F(w-4).1,4X$
$10^{d-1} \leqslant v < 10^{d}$	$F(w-4).0,4X$
Otherwise	$Ew.d$

The G field descriptor is used to obtain the readability of the F field descriptor while eliminating the chance of obtaining a "too large" or "too small" error indication during output.

If N is the magnitude of the internal data item and if $N < .01$ or $N \geqslant 10^{d}$, then $Gw.d$ is equivalent to $kPEw.d$, where k is the current scale factor.

A variation to the G field descriptor takes the form:

$$Gw.dEe$$

For input, the $Gw.dEe$ field descriptor is treated identically to that of the $Gw.d$ field descriptor. For output, the $Gw.dEe$ field is treated identically to $Fw.dEe$ if $N \geqslant 0.1$ and $N < 10^{d}$, and is identical to $Ew.dEe$ if $N < 0.1$ or $N \geqslant 10^{d}$.

12.3.1.7 Scale Factor

A scale factor descriptor takes the form:

$$kP$$

where the scale factor k is an unsigned or a negative integer constant. With F field descriptors, the scale factor has the following effect for input and output:

$$\text{External value} = \text{internal value} * 10^k$$

For example, the statements:

$$A=0.123$$
$$\text{WRITE}(6,9002)A$$
$$9002 \quad \text{FORMAT}(1H,2PF5.1)$$

would cause A to be printed as:

$$\not b 12.3$$

If an input field for F editing contains an exponent, then the scale factor is ignored. With the E and D field descriptors, the scale factor is ignored for input, if an exponent is used, and scales the fraction without changing the magnitude for output. More specifically, the output fraction is multiplied by 10^k and the exponent is adjusted accordingly. For example, the statements:

$$A= 12.345$$
$$B= A$$
$$\text{WRITE}(6,9003)A,B$$
$$9003 \quad \text{FORMAT}(1H,E12.5,1PE12.5)$$

would produce the result:

$$\not b 0.12345E \ 02 \not b \not b 1.2345E \ 01$$

With the G field descriptor, input is handled as follows: (1) If the input field does not contain an exponent, it is processed in the same fashion as format F input; and (2) if the input field contains an exponent, then the scale factor has no effect. For format G output, the scale factor has no effect unless the data item is outside the range of format F output and format E conversion is used. If format E output conversion is required, the scale factor causes the same result as with format E output conversion.

The scale factor is said to be established once it is used with an appropriate field descriptor.   Once a scale factor is established, it applies to the interpretation of subsequent F, E, D, and G field descriptors until another scale factor is encountered.   The effect of a scale factor can be effectively nullified with a scale factor of the form:

$$0P(\text{i.e., "zero P"})$$

Therefore, if a scale factor is to affect only one field, the 0P scale factor should accompany the next F,E,D, or G field descriptor to be interpreted.

12.3.2 Logical Editing

The *L field descriptor* is used for logical data and takes the form:

$$Lw$$

where *w* is the width of the field.   The input field consists of optional blanks, followed by an optional decimal point, followed by T or F, followed by optional characters, for true and false, respectively. The logical constants .TRUE. and .FALSE. are acceptable input forms for true and false, respectively.   For output, the field consists of either a T or an F, for true and false, respectively, followed by $w-1$ blank characters.

12.3.3 Character Editing

Character editing in FORTRAN 77 can take either of three forms: apostrophe editing, H editing, and A editing.   Apostrophe and H editing are a means of including descriptive information in a FORMAT statement and can be used *only* for output.

12.3.3.1 Apostrophe Editing

Apostrophe editing takes the form of a character constant and causes characters to be written from the format statement, as suggested in the following example:

$$\text{WRITE(N,9000)A}$$
$$9000 \quad \text{FORMAT(' SUM =',F6.2)}$$

The width of the output field is the number of characters contained in the character constant, excluding the enclosing apostrophes. The apostrophe edit descriptor does not correspond to an output list item.

   Within the apostrophe edit descriptor, an apostrophe is represented by two successive apostrophe characters.

12.3.3.2 H Editing

The H field descriptor is used for Hollerith data and takes the following form:

$$w \text{ H } \underbrace{xxx...x}_{w \text{ characters}}$$

where w is an unsigned integer constant that denotes the number of Hollerith characters that comprise the Hollerith literal, which follows the letter H. As with the apostrophe edit descriptor, the H field descriptor does not require a corresponding list item, demonstrated as follows:

WRITE(N,9010)A
9010   FORMAT(7H SUM = ,F6.2)

With earlier versions of the FORTRAN language, the H field descriptor could be used for input wherein characters from the input record were placed in the H field in the FORMAT statement. Those characters could subsequently be used as an output descriptor—such as a column heading. *This is not the case in FORTRAN 77 and the H field descriptor can only be used for output.*

12.3.3.3 A Editing

The A field descriptor is used for the editing of character data and has the following form:

Aw

where w is the width of the external data field. The A field descriptor operates as follows (g is the number of characters that are stored in the corresponding character variable or character array element):

1. For input, if $w \geq g$, the rightmost g characters are taken from the external input field; if $w < g$, the w characters are left justified in the character data item followed (in the word) by $g-w$ trailing blank characters.
2. For output, if $w > g$, the external output field consists of $w-g$ blank characters followed by the g characters from the character data item; if $w \leq g$, the external output field consists of the leftmost w characters from the character data item.

A variation to the A field descriptor takes the form:

$$A$$

with the field width omitted. This form may be used for output editing and the width of the external data field is the length of the character output list item.

12.3.4 Positional Editing

Positional edit control descriptors can be used to specify a position in a data record from which the next input or output editing is to take place. This facility permits an external character position to be established and allows portions of a record to be reprocessed or skipped for input. For output, the facility can be used to specify precision editing and field alignment.

12.3.4.1 X Editing

The character position specified by the X edit control descriptor specifies a position forward from the current position. Thus, the X edit control descriptor is used to skip characters on the external medium for input and output. The form of the X edit control descriptor is:

$$wX$$

where w is an unsigned nonzero integer constant that denotes the number of characters to be skipped. For input, w character positions of the input record are skipped, regardless of their contents. For output, the output record for formatted output is initially filled with blanks. Data fields are moved into the output record from left to right as conversions and editing are performed under format control. Use of the X edit control descriptor simply moves a pointer the indicated number of positions to the right, resulting in blank characters in the output record.

12.3.4.2 T Editing

The T edit control descriptor specifies an absolute position in an input or output record; the specified position may be backward or forward from the current position and effectively moves the current position pointer to the specified character position. The form of the T edit control descriptor is:

$$Tc$$

where c is an unsigned nonzero integer constant which specifies that the next character transmitted to or from an external data record would take place at the cth character position.

12.3.4.3 TL Editing

The TL edit control descriptor is used to move the current position pointer backward. The form of the TL edit control descriptor is:

$$TLs$$

where s is an unsigned integer constant specifying the number of character positions the current position pointer should be moved backward (i.e., to the left) in the external data record.

12.3.4.4 TR Editing

The TR edit control descriptor is used to move the current position pointer forward. The form of the TR edit control descriptor is:

$$TRs$$

where s is an unsigned integer constant specifying the number of character positions the current position pointer should be moved forward (i.e., to the right) in the external data record.

12.3.5 Record Control Editing

Record edit control descriptors are used to terminate the processing of the current data record. Edit control descriptors supplement the case given earlier wherein a format specification is exhausted before all input/output list items are processed. In this case, format control is returned to the last open parenthesis and the input/output system goes to the next record.

12.3.5.1 Slash Editing

A *slash* (/) placed in a format specification as a distinct edit control descriptor or as a separator causes the processor to go to the next external data record. For input, a new record is read and the current position pointer is set to its first character position. For output, n slashes in succession causes $n-1$ blank lines to be generated. As with input, the current position pointer is set to the first character position of the new output record. Through the use of two or more successive slashes in a format specification, entire records can be skipped for input and records containing no characters can be generated for output.

With direct access files, the next record is identified by increasing the record count by one.

12.3.5.2 Colon Editing

A *colon* (:) placed in a format specification as a distinct edit control descriptor or as a separator causes the processor to terminate the output operation if it is encountered during format control and no items remain in the output list. If the colon is encountered in an input operation or if additional list items remain for output, the colon is ignored.

12.3.6 Sign Control Editing

Sign control edit descriptors can be used to govern the placement of a plus sign in a numeric output field, and affect the following field descriptors: I, F, E, D, and G. As with the scale factor, a sign control edit descriptor remains in effect, after being specified, until another sign control edit descriptor is encountered during format control. The S, SP, and SS edit control descriptors are ignored for input operations.

12.3.6.1 SP Editing

The SP edit control descriptor specifies that the processor should insert a plus sign in any character position that contains an optional plus sign.

12.3.6.2 SS Editing

The SS edit control descriptor specifies that the processor should not insert a plus sign in any character position that contains an optional plus sign.

12.3.6.3 S Editing

The S edit control descriptor specifies that the processor should return to the normal mode for inserting plus signs in numeric output fields.

12.3.7 Blank Control Editing

Blank control edit descriptors specify how blank characters in numeric input fields, other than leading blanks, should be interpreted by the processor. Blank control is governed by the "BLANK=" specifier in the OPEN statement or assumes a default value. The specified option for blank control takes affect at the start of execution of a formatted input statement. The option stays in affect until either a BN or a BZ edit control specifier is encountered during format control.

12.3.7.1 BN Editing

A BN edit control descriptor causes the processor to ignore blank characters in a numeric input field and to right justify remaining characters, as though the blanks that were ignored were leading blanks. A field of all blanks has a zero value.

12.3.7.2 BZ Editing

A BZ edit control descriptor causes the processor to treat blank characters in a numeric input field as zeros.

12.3.8 Field Separators

A comma is used as a separator between field and edit control descriptors. It may be omitted before and after slash and colon edit control descriptors, such that the slash and colon in themselves become separators, and between a P edit control descriptor and a following F, E, D, and G field descriptor.

In most implementations of FORTRAN, a field separator is not needed after the wX and wH '. . .' field descriptors. This facility is not covered in the FORTRAN 77 standard.

12.3.9 Repeat Count

A nonzero unsigned integer constant preceding a field descriptor is a repeat count that denotes a repeat count for the field descriptor or group format specification. Thus, a specification of the form 3I2 is equivalent to I2, I2, I2. The repeat count also applies to a parenthesized list of field and edit control descriptors. Thus, 3(I4,F10.2) is equivalent to I4,F10.2,I4,F10.2,I4,F10.2.

12.3.10 Group Format Specification

A parenthesized list of field and edit control descriptors is referred to as a *group format specification*, which can be used with the repeat count and for record control. An example serves to demonstrate the concept. It is desired to read a value N with I4 format from a single card and then read N values from subsequent cards in format F12.6 with six values per card. The following statements could be used:

```
      REAL A(100)
      READ(5,9000)N,(A(I),I=1,N)
 9000 FORMAT(I4/(6F12.6))
```

The example depicts a slash to go to the next card, a repetition factor, a parenthesized list, and a return to the last open parenthesis.

12.4 LIST DIRECTED FORMATTING

List directed formatting permits formatted input and output without the use of a format specification. On the external medium, data values are separated by a comma or by one or more successive spaces. A comma can optionally be preceded and followed by spaces. For input, a data value must have the same type as the list element to which it corresponds. The data values are written as FORTRAN 77 constants and are interpreted from left to right in the input record and are used to define the list elements in a READ statement with the format identifier specified by an asterisk. Values can be continued on successive input records and a null value is denoted by successive commas. A slash in an input record as a separator (i.e., not in a character constant) terminates the execution of an input list and assigns null values to remaining elements in the input list. Assignment of a null value to an input element has no effect and does not cause it to become defined or become undefined.

Input values may be written using repetition specifications of the following forms:

$$r*c$$
$$r*$$

where r is an unsigned nonzero integer constant, denoting a repetition factor, and c is a FORTRAN 77 constant. The form $r*c$ specifies r repetitions of the constant c while $r*$ specifies r null values.

For output, the specified list elements are written to one or more output records in a suitable format that is implementation-defined. Successive data values are separated by commas or blanks.

13 | PROGRAM STRUCTURE

13.1 OVERVIEW

The elements from which a program is comprised can include the following:

1. One main program
2. Zero or more intrinsic functions
3. Zero or more external procedures
4. Zero or more BLOCK DATA program units

The main program and external procedures may additionally define and reference a one-line internal function known as a statement function. The BLOCK DATA program unit was covered previously and is not covered in this chapter.

13.2 MAIN PROGRAM

A main program is a program unit that is not an external procedure or a BLOCK DATA program unit. The main program receives control of the processor when an executable program is loaded for execution. There can be only one main program in an executable program and that main program is identified by the fact that it does not have a FUNCTION, SUBROUTINE, or BLOCK DATA statement as its initial statement. A main program may have a PROGRAM statement as its initial statement.

13.2.1 PROGRAM Statement

The form of a PROGRAM statement is:

$$PROGRAM \; pgm$$

where *pgm* is the symbolic name of the main program. The optional PROGRAM statement defines a symbolic name which must be a unique external name and must not be the same as any internal name in the main program.

13.2.2 Structure of a Main Program

A main program may be composed of any set of FORTRAN 77 statements except the FUNCTION, SUBROUTINE, or BLOCK DATA statements, mentioned above. The execution of a STOP or END statement in a main program terminates execution of the program, as does the execution of a STOP statement in any program unit of the executable program. A SAVE statement in a main program does not affect the status of variables or arrays since all data entities defined in the main program have a static storage class.

13.3 INTRINSIC FUNCTIONS

An intrinsic function is supplied by the processor and is generated as an in-line function or as a library function. The intrinsic functions defined in the standard document as being a part of FORTRAN 77 are listed in Appendix A. Sample intrinsic functions are: ABS for absolute value, INT for conversion to integer, SIN for trigonometric sign, and SQRT for square root.

13.3.1 Referencing an Intrinsic Function

A reference to an intrinsic function takes the following form:

$$fun \; (a[,a])$$

where *fun* is the generic or the specific name of the intrinsic function and *a* is an actual argument. The actual arguments *a* constitute the argument list and must agree in order, number, and type with the specifications given in Appendix A. An actual argument may be any valid expression except a character expression that contains concatenation to an operand with a length attribute specified with an asterisk.

An intrinsic function reference may be used as a primary in an expression and is invoked during the evaluation of the expression at the point of reference during program execution. The following statement, for example, contains a reference to an intrinsic function:

$$HYP = SQRT(X**2+Y**2)$$

The results of the various intrinsic functions are given in Appendix A.

13.3.2 Generic Names

A *generic name* is the single name given to a class of objects. With regard to intrinsic functions in FORTRAN 77, functions that perform the same mathematical function, such as absolute value, are given a single name, such as ABS. Therefore, the generic name may be used—regardless of the data type of the argument(s). When a generic name is referenced, the processor substitutes a function call to a specific name, depending upon the data type of the argument(s).

13.3.3 Operational Conventions

Except for type conversion functions, the data type of the result of an intrinsic function is the same as the argument(s). If more than one argument is permitted or required, then all arguments must have the same type. The data type of a specific or generic name of an intrinsic function may not be changed with an IMPLICIT statement.

If it is desired to include the name of an intrinsic function as an actual argument in an external procedure reference, the specific name of the function must be used and that name must appear in an INTRINSIC statement in the calling program unit. The names of intrinsic functions for type conversion and for computing the largest or smallest value may not be used as actual arguments.

13.4 STATEMENT FUNCTION

A *statement function* is a one-line defined function that is internal to the program unit in which it is defined. The following statement, for example, would be a statement function:

$$ROOT(A,B,C) = (-B+SQRT(B**2-4.0*A*C))/(2.0*A)$$

provided that other operational conventions were satisfied. A statement function is referenced in the same manner as an intrinsic function is referenced, and it returns a value to the point of reference in the execution of a program unit. Thus, a statement function reference can be used as a primary in an expression and it has a data type based on its name, which may be declared implicitly or explicitly.

13.4.1 Definition of a Statement Function

A statement function definition is made through a statement function statement, which has the form:

$$fun([d[,d] \ldots])=e$$

where d is a dummy argument and e is a FORTRAN 77 expression. The expression fun is the symbolic name of the function and the data type of fun and e may be different. The rules of assignment apply here. Each dummy argument is a variable name, which has a data type, and is referenced in e. All arguments need not have the same data type. A specific dummy argument may appear only once in the argument list of a statement function definition. Moreover, a variable name that serves as a dummy argument may not be used in the same program unit as an actual variable. However, the same dummy argument may be used in more than one statement function statement in the same program unit.

The name of a statement function and of a variable that serves as a dummy argument may appear in a type statement. The name of a statement function may not be used to name any other constituent in a program unit, except that the same name may be used as the name of a labeled common block.

The primaries in the expression e are not limited to variable names in the argument list, but may include other entities that are defined when the statement function is referenced. More specifically, the primaries of e may include:

1. Dummy argument names
2. Constants
3. Parameters

4. Variable references
5. Array element references
6. Intrinsic function references
7. External function references
8. Dummy procedure references
9. References to other statement functions
10. An expression, composed of (1) through (9), enclosed in parentheses

If a statement function reference is used in *e*, then it must have been defined previously and it must not be the name of the statement function being defined. The latter statement should be interpreted to mean that recursion is not permitted.

A statement function statement must precede all executable statements in a program unit.

13.4.2 Statement Function Reference

A statement function is referenced by using its name with actual arguments, if any, enclosed in parentheses as a primary in an expression. The form of a statement function reference is:

$$fun([exp[,exp] \ldots])$$

where *fun* is the statement function name and *exp* are expressions evaluated at the point of reference. The value of each expression must agree in order, number, and type with the corresponding dummy argument in the statement function statement.

In the execution of a statement function, the actual argument expressions are evaluated and passed to the function. The expression *e*, of the statement function statement, is then evaluated and the resulting value is converted, if necessary, to the data type of *fun*. This value is returned as the value of the statement function reference.

An actual argument expression may not involve a concatenation in which the length attribute of one of the operands was declared with an asterisk.

13.5 EXTERNAL PROCEDURES

An external procedure is a program unit that exists as an independent entity; it can be coded in the FORTRAN 77 language or by some other means. This presentation covers only external procedures written in FORTRAN 77; however, the new FORTRAN standard, as well as the 1966 standard, permits external procedures to be represented in other languages that are acceptable to the processor.*

13.5.1 Kinds of External Procedures

Two kinds of external procedures exist in FORTRAN 77: function subprograms and subroutine subprograms. For convenience, they are commonly referred to as "functions" and "subroutines," respectively.

A function subprogram is composed of a FUNCTION statement, followed by a program body, which terminates with an END statement; it has the following "general" form:

$$\text{FUNCTION name } ([a[,a] \dots])$$

$$\left. \begin{matrix} . \\ . \\ . \end{matrix} \right\} \text{ Body of the function}$$

$$\text{END}$$

A function subprogram may be referenced as a primary in an expression that is contained in a distinct program unit but is part of the same executable program.

A subroutine subprogram is composed of a SUBROUTINE statement, followed by a program body, which terminates with an END statement; it has the following "general" form:

$$\text{SUBROUTINE name } [([a[,a] \dots])]$$

$$\left. \begin{matrix} . \\ . \\ . \end{matrix} \right\} \text{ Body of the function}$$

$$\text{END}$$

A subroutine subprogram may be referenced with the CALL statement that is contained in a distinct program unit but is part of the same executable program.

---

*In this instance, "processor" refers to the total operating environment including the operating system and associated language processors.

13.5.2 Execution of an External Procedure

An external procedure is executed as follows:

1. The external procedure is invoked through a function reference or through a CALL statement, depending upon whether the procedure is a function or a subroutine, respectively.
2. Expressions that constitute actual arguments are evaluated.
3. The actual arguments from the calling program unit are associated with dummy arguments in the external procedure.
4. The statements that comprise the external procedure are executed in an order based on the execution control sequence of the program unit.
5. Program control is returned to the calling program unit when either a RETURN statement is executed or the execution control in the external procedure flows into the END statement.

The name of a function subprogram must appear as a variable at least once in the subprogram. During each execution of the function, this variable must be defined at least once. Once the variable is defined, it may be referenced elsewhere in the function and become redefined. When program control is returned to the calling program, it is this value that is returned as the value of the function reference. A function subprogram always returns a scalar value to the point of invocation in the calling program unit. The data type of the function reference must be the same as that of the function name in the referenced function, and in the case of a character data type, the length attributes must be the same. If the length of the character variable, representing the function name in the referenced function, is specified as an asterisk enclosed in parentheses, then the function assumes the length specified in the referencing program unit. In the function, a character variable representing the function name, may not appear as an operand in a concatenation operation, but may be defined in an assignment statement.

Since a subroutine is not used as a primary in an expression, it does not return an explicit value to the point of reference. However, the subroutine and the function, as well, can return values to the calling program unit by defining one or more of their dummy arguments during the course of execution.

13.5.3 FUNCTION Statement

The form of the FUNCTION statement is:

$$[typ] \text{ FUNCTION } fun([d[,d] \ldots])$$

The *typ* option has one of the following forms:

> INTEGER
> REAL
> DOUBLE PRECISION
> COMPLEX
> LOGICAL
> CHARACTER [*len*]

and specifies the data type of the function name, which determines the value returned to the calling program. Each of the above data type attributes was introduced earlier in Chapter Seven, "Specification Statements." The object *fun* is the symbolic name of the external function and unless specified otherwise, implicit typing conventions apply. It is an external name and in a given executable program, it must be unique. Thus, for example, two external procedures may not have the same symbolic name. The type specification may be omitted from the FUNCTION statement and the function name may be specified in a type statement in the same program unit. However, the name of the function may not appear in both the FUNCTION statement and in a type statement. The following statements, for example:

> FUNCTION CROOT(A,B,C)
> COMPLEX CROOT

are equivalent to:

> COMPLEX FUNCTION CROOT(A,B,C)

The dummy argument *d* may be a variable name, array name, or dummy procedure name. A symbolic name appearing as a dummy argument in a FUNCTION statement is known only in that program unit and must not appear in any of the following statements in the body of the function: EQUIVALENCE, PARAMETER, SAVE, INTRINSIC, DATA, or COMMON. The name of a labeled common block may be the same as a dummy argument.

13.5.4 Referencing an External Function

A reference to an external function takes the following form:

$$fun([a[,a]\ldots])$$

where *fun* is the symbolic name of the external function and *a* is an actual argument. The actual arguments *a* constitute an argument list and must agree in order, number, and type with the corresponding dummy arguments in the referenced function.

If a dummy procedure name is specified as a dummy argument in the referenced function, then an actual procedure name must be supplied in the corresponding position in the argument list of the function. If the dummy procedure name specifies a function, then the data type of the function supplied in the reference must agree with the data type of the dummy procedure name in the referenced function. In the case of an intrinsic function, a specific function name must be supplied. If the dummy procedure name specifies a subroutine name, then the concept of a data type does not apply.

An actual argument in a function reference must be one of the following:

1. An expression, excepting a character expression containing a concatenation operation in which one of the operands is a character variable with a length attribute specified as an asterisk in parentheses
2. An array name
3. An intrinsic function name
4. An external procedure name
5. A dummy procedure name

Use of the dummy procedure name permits actual procedure names to be passed through several levels of program units. Additional information on arguments is covered later.

13.5.5 SUBROUTINE Statement

The form of the SUBROUTINE statement is:

$$\text{SUBROUTINE } sub\,[([d[,d]\ldots])]$$

The object *sub* is the external name of the subroutine of which the SUBROUTINE statement is its first statement, and *d* is a dummy argument that takes one of the following forms for a sub-routine:

1. Variable name
2. Array name
3. Dummy procedure name
4. An asterisk

The asterisk denotes an alternate return, suggested by the following example. Consider the subroutine defined as follows:

SUBROUTINE BSCALE(A,B,C,*,*,*)

. . .

IF (A .LT. 0.0) RETURN 1
IF (A .EQ. 0.0) RETURN 2
RETURN 3
END

and the subroutine call:

CALL BSCALE(X+Y,LOG(Z), 1.54,*1000,*2000,*3000)

In the CALL statement, 1000, 2000, and 3000 are statement numbers of executable statements in the calling program. Now in subroutine BSCALE, if the value of A is less than zero, then program control via the RETURN 1 statement is made to the statement number specified as the actual argument corresponding to the first asterisk. In effect, control is returned via the alternate return to statement numbered 1000 in the calling program. Similarly, if A is equal to zero, the control is effectively returned to statement numbered 2000 in the calling program. Otherwise, the RETURN 3 statement in the subroutine causes control to be returned to the actual argument corresponding to the third asterisk, which is statement numbered 3000 in this case.

If no arguments are to be used with a subroutine, then either of the following forms can be used:

SUBROUTINE *sub*

or

SUBROUTINE *sub* ( )

13.5.6 CALL Statement

A subroutine is referenced in a calling program unit with the CALL statement that has the following form:

$$\text{CALL } sub \, [([a[,a] \ldots])]$$

where *sub* is the symbolic name of the subroutine and *a* is an actual argument. The actual arguments *a* constitute an argument list and must agree in order, number, and type with the corresponding dummy arguments in the referenced subroutine.

If a dummy procedure name is specified as a dummy argument in the referenced subroutine, then an actual procedure name must be supplied in the corresponding position in the argument list of the CALL statement. If the dummy procedure name specifies a function, then the data type of the function supplied in the CALL statement must agree with the data type of the dummy procedure name in the referenced subroutine. In the case of an intrinsic function, a specific function name must be supplied. If the dummy procedure name specifies a subroutine name, then the concept of a data type does not apply.

If an asterisk is specified as a dummy argument in the referenced subroutine, then a statement number must be supplied in the corresponding position in the argument list of the CALL statement.

A Hollerith constant may be used as an actual argument in a CALL statement and the corresponding dummy argument must be of type integer, real, or logical. The Hollerith data type has been deleted in FORTRAN 77 and the above information is included for organizations desiring to extend the language by incorporating the Hollerith data type.

An actual argument in an argument list of a CALL statement must be one of the following:

1. An expression, excepting a character expression containing a concatenation operation in which one of the operands is a character variable with a length attribute specified as an asterisk in parentheses
2. An array name
3. An intrinsic function name
4. An external procedure name

5. A dummy procedure name
6. An alternate return specifier of the form *s, where s is the statement number of an executable statement

As with the external function reference, the use of a dummy procedure name permits actual procedure names to be passed through several levels of program units. Additional information on arguments is covered later.

A subroutine that has been defined without arguments, i.e., either of the forms sub or sub( ), may be referenced by a call statement of the form CALL sub, or alternately CALL sub( ). The two forms are completely interchangeable in both the SUBROUTINE and CALL statements.

13.5.7 ENTRY Statement

The ENTRY statement can be used to specify a secondary entry point in a function or a subroutine. The ENTRY statement must appear after the FUNCTION or SUBROUTINE statement in an external procedure and has the following form:

$$\text{ENTRY } en \, [([d[,d] \ldots])]$$

where en is the external symbolic name of an entry point and d is a dummy argument. If an ENTRY statement is included in a function, then it is treated exactly like a FUNCTION statement. If an ENTRY statement is included in a subroutine, then it is treated exactly like a SUBROUTINE statement.

A secondary entry in a function must be referenced as a function; a secondary entry in a subroutine must be referenced with a CALL statement. The dummy argument list in an ENTRY statement need not agree in order, number, type, and in name with the FUNCTION or SUBROUTINE statement serving as the first statement of the external procedure in which the ENTRY statement is included. However, when a secondary entry point is referenced, the actual argument list must agree in order, number, and type with the dummy argument list in the ENTRY statement.

13.5.8 RETURN Statement

The RETURN statement causes program control to be returned to the referencing program unit and has the following forms:

RETURN

and

RETURN [*e*]

The second form may only appear in a subroutine and the integer expression *e* specifies an alternate return, as covered above. If $1 \leqslant e \leqslant n$, where *n* is the number of asterisks in the SUBROUTINE or ENTRY statement, then program control is returned to the statement number, supplied as an actual parameter in a CALL statement, corresponding to the eth asterisk in the SUBROUTINE or ENTRY statement. If the value of *e* is less than 1 or greater than *n*, then a normal return is executed.

The execution of a RETURN statement (or a default END statement) causes all entities in an external procedure to become undefined, except as specified below:

1. Those entities specified in a SAVE statement
2. Those entities in blank common
3. Those entities initialized in a DATA statement that have neither been redefined nor become undefined
4. Those entities in a labeled common block that is specified in the same external procedure that includes the RETURN statement and is also specified, directly or indirectly, in other program units that reference the external procedure

Therefore, any entity specified in a labeled common block in a program unit cannot become undefined through the execution of a RETURN statement in a subordinate program unit.

13.5.9 END Statement

The form of an END statement is:

END

The END statement serves as the physical end of a program unit and causes the following actions to be performed if program control flows into it:

1. If the END statement is in the main program, then execution is terminated.

2. If the END statement is in an external procedure, then an implicit return is executed to the referencing program unit.

The effect of an implicit return is the same as if a RETURN statement were executed.

13.5.10 Passing Array Arguments to Subprograms

An array can be passed to a function or subroutine as an actual argument provided that the corresponding dummy argument is also an array, declared in a DIMENSION or type statement, but not in a COMMON statement. The size of the array in the calling program unit must be smaller than or equal to the size of the corresponding dummy array in the function or subroutine.* Alternately, the array in the function or subroutine may have adjustable dimensions.

The following example which yields the transpose of a matrix depicts the use of adjustable dimensions:

```
     SUBROUTINE TRANSP(A,M,N,B)
     REAL A(M,N),B(N,M)
     DO 50 I=1,M
     DO 50 J=1,N
  50 B(J,I)=A(I,J)
     RETURN
     END
```

It would be with a program segment such as:

```
     REAL PMAT(15,10),RMAT(10,15)
     . . .
     CALL TRANSP (PMAT,15,10,RMAT)
```

The specification of adjustable dimensions in a function or subroutine is the only case in which an array declarator may include a variable. When an adjustable array is specified, at least one dimension must be specified by a variable that serves as a dummy argument or by a variable in a common block.

---

*The array dimensions need not be the same in the calling program unit and the referenced function or subroutine since an array occupies contiguous storage units.

When an array name or an element of an array is passed to a function or subroutine, it is the address of that entity that is passed and not the data values. Therefore, an association may be established between a part of an array in the calling program unit and a dummy array in a function or subroutine.

REFERENCES

American National Standards Committee, *American National Standard Programming Language FORTRAN* (FORTRAN 77), Document X3J3/90, X3 Secretariat, CBEMA/Standards, 1828 L Street, N.W., Washington, D.C., 20036.

American Standard FORTRAN, New York: American Standards Association, Inc., 1966.

"Draft Proposed ANS FORTRAN," *SIGPLAN Notices*, **11** (3), March, 1976.

IBM System/360 and System/370 FORTRAN IV Language, IBM Corporation, New York, New York, Form #GC28-6515, 1974.

Katzan, H., *Introduction to Programming Languages*, Philadelphia: Auerbach Publishers Inc., 1973.

Woolley, John D., "FORTRAN: A Comparison of the New Proposed Language (1976) to the old Standard (1966)," *SIGPLAN Notices*, **12** (7), July, 1977, p. 112-125.

APPENDIX A
INTRINSIC FUNCTIONS

Intrinsic Function	Definition	Number of Arguments	Generic Name	Specific Name	Type of	
					Argument	Function
Type Conversion	Conversion to Integer int (a)	1	INT	–	Integer	Integer
				INT	Real	Integer
				IFIX	Real	Integer
				IDINT	Double	Integer
				–	Complex	Integer
	Conversion to Real	1	REAL	REAL	Integer	Real
				FLOAT	Integer	Real
				–	Real	Real
				SNGL	Double	Real
				–	Complex	Real
	Conversion to Double	1	DBLE	–	Integer	Double
				–	Real	Double
				–	Double	Double
				–	Complex	Double
	Conversion to Complex	1 or 2	CMPLX	–	Integer	Complex
				–	Real	Complex
				–	Double	Complex
				–	Complex	Complex
	Conversion to Integer	1	–	ICHAR	Character	Integer
	Conversion to Character	1	–	CHAR	Integer	Character

Intrinsic Function	Definition	Number of Arguments	Generic Name	Specific Name	Type of Argument	Type of Function
Truncation	int (a)	1	AINT	AINT	Real	Real
				DINT	Double	Double
Nearest Whole Number	int $(a+.5)$ if $a \geqslant 0$ int $(a-.5)$ if $a < 0$	1	ANINT	ANINT	Real	Real
				DNINT	Double	Double
Nearest Integer	int $(a+.5)$ if $a \geqslant 0$ int $(a-.5)$ if $a < 0$	1	NINT	NINT	Real	Integer
				IDNINT	Double	Integer
Absolute Value	$\|a\|$	1	ABS	IABS	Integer	Integer
				ABS	Real	Real
				DABS	Double	Double
	$(ar^2 + ai^2)^{1/2}$			CABS	Complex	Real
Remaindering	$a_1 - $ int $(a_1/a_2)*a_2$	2	MOD	MOD	Integer	Integer
				AMOD	Real	Real
				DMOD	Double	Double
Transfer of Sign	$\|a_1\|$ if $a_2 \geqslant 0$ $-\|a_1\|$ if $a_2 < 0$	2	SIGN	ISIGN	Integer	Integer
				SIGN	Real	Real
				DSIGN	Double	Double
Positive Difference	$a_1 - a_2$ if $a_1 > a_2$ 0 if $a_1 \leqslant a_2$	2	DIM	IDIM	Integer	Integer
				DIM	Real	Real
				DDIM	Double	Double
Double Precision Product	a_1*a_2	2	—	DPROD	Real	Double
Choosing Largest Value	max $(a_1, a_2, \ldots)$	$\geqslant 2$	MAX	MAXO	Integer	Integer
				AMAX1	Real	Real
				DMAX1	Double	Double
			—	AMAX0	Integer	Real
			—	MAX1	Real	Integer
Choosing Smallest Value	min $(a_1, a_2, \ldots)$	$\geqslant 2$	MIN	MINO	Integer	Integer
				AMIN1	Real	Real
				DMIN1	Double	Double
			—	AMIN0	Integer	Real
			—	MIN1	Real	Integer
Length	Length of Character Entity	1	—	LEN	Character	Integer
Index of a Substring	Location of Substring a_2 in String a_1	2	—	INDEX	Character	Integer

Intrinsic Function	Definition	Number of Arguments	Generic Name	Specific Name	Type of Argument	Function
Imaginary Part of Complex Argument	ai	1	–	AIMAG	Complex	Real
Conjugate of a Complex Argument	$(ar, -ai)$	1	–	CONJG	Complex	Complex
Square Root	$(a)^{1/2}$	1	SQRT	SQRT DSQRT CSQRT	Real Double Complex	Real Double Complex
Exponential	$e**a$	1	EXP	EXP DEXP CEXP	Real Double Complex	Real Double Complex
Natural Logarithm	$\log(a)$	1	LOG	ALOG DLOG CLOG	Real Double Complex	Real Double Complex
Common Logarithm	$\log 10(a)$	1	LOG10	ALOG10 DLOG10	Real Double	Real Double
Sine	$\sin(a)$	1	SIN	SIN DSIN CSIN	Real Double Complex	Real Double Complex
Cosine	$\cos(a)$	1	COS	COS DCOS CCOS	Real Double Complex	Real Double Complex
Tangent	$\tan(a)$	1	TAN	TAN DTAN	Real Double	Real Double
Arcsine	$\arcsin(a)$	1	ASIN	ASIN DASIN	Real Double	Real Double
Arccosine	$\arccos(a)$	1	ACOS	ACOS DACOS	Real Double	Real Double
Arctangent	$\arctan(a)$	1	ATAN	ATAN DATAN	Real Double	Real Double
	$\arctan(a_1/a_2)$	2	ATAN2	ATAN2 DATAN2	Real Double	Real Double
Hyperbolic Sine	$\sinh(a)$	1	SINH	SINH DSINH	Real Double	Real Double
Hyperbolic Cosine	$\cosh(a)$	1	COSH	COSH DCOSH	Real Double	Real Double
Hyperbolic Tangent	$\tanh(a)$	1	TANH	TANH DTANH	Real Double	Real Double

APPENDIX B
SYNTAX OF FORTRAN STATEMENTS

Form	Descriptive Heading
ASSIGN s TO i	Statement Label Assignment Statement
BACKSPACE u BACKSPACE (alist)	File Positioning Statements
BLOCK DATA [sub]	BLOCK DATA Statement
CALL sub [([a [,c] ...])]	Subroutine Reference: CALL Statement
CHARACTER [*len[,]] nam [,nam] ...	Character Type-Statement
CLOSE (cllist)	CLOSE Statement
COMMON [/[cb]/]nlist[[,]/cb]/nlist] ...	COMMON Statement
COMPLEX v [,v] ...	Complex Type-Statement
CONTINUE	CONTINUE Statement
DATA nlist/clist/[[,]nlist/clist/]...	DATA Statement
DIMENSION a(d) [,a(d)] ...	DIMENSION Statement
DO s [,] i=e_1,e_2 [,e_3]	DO Statement
DOUBLE PRECISION v [,v] ...	Double Precision Type-Statement
ELSE	ELSE Statement
ELSE IF (e) THEN	ELSE IF Statement
END	END Statement
END IF	END IF Statement
ENDFILE u ENDFILE (alist)	File Positioning Statements
ENTRY en [([d [,d] ...])]	ENTRY Statement
EQUIVALENCE (nlist) [,(nlist)] ...	EQUIVALENCE Statement
EXTERNAL proc [,proc] ...	EXTERNAL Statement

Form	Descriptive Heading
FORMAT fs	FORMAT Statement
fun ([d [,d] ...]) = e	Statement Function Statement
[typ] FUNCTION fun ([d [,d] ...])	FUNCTION Statement
GO TO i [[,[(s [,s] ...)]	Assigned GO TO Statement
GO TO s	Unconditional GO TO Statement
GO TO (s [,s] ...)[,] i	Computed GO TO Statement
IF (e) st	Logical IF Statement
IF (e) s_1, s_2, s_3	Arithmetic IF Statement
IF (e) THEN	Block IF Statement
IMPLICIT typ (a [,a] ...) [,typ (a [,a] ...)] ...	IMPLICIT Statement
INQUIRE (iflist)	INQUIRE by File Statement
INQUIRE (iulist)	INQUIRE by Unit Statement
INTEGER v [,v] ...	Integer Type-Statement
INTRINSIC fun [,fun] ...	INTRINSIC Statement
LOGICAL v [,v] ...	Logical Type-Statement
OPEN (olist)	OPEN Statement
PARAMETER (p=e [,p=e] ...)	PARAMETER Statement
PAUSE [n]	PAUSE Statement
PRINT f [,iolist]	Data Transfer Output Statement
PROGRAM pgm	PROGRAM Statement
READ (cilist) [iolist]	Data Transfer Input Statement
READ f [,iolist]	Data Transfer Input Statement
REAL v [,v] ...	Real Type-Statement
RETURN [e]	RETURN Statement
REWIND u REWIND (alist)	File Positioning Statements
SAVE [a [,a] ...]	SAVE Statement
STOP [n]	STOP Statement
SUBROUTINE sub [([d [,d] ...])]	SUBROUTINE Statement
v = e	Arithmetic Assignment Statement
v = e	Logical Assignment Statement
v = e	Character Assignment Statement
WRITE (cilist) [iolist]	Data Transfer Output Statement

APPENDIX C
SYNTAX CHART OF FORTRAN 77

1   executable_program:

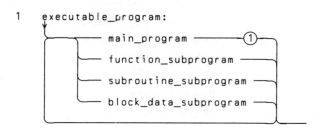

    (1)   An executable program must contain one and only one main program.

        An executable program may contain external procedures specified by means other than FORTRAN.

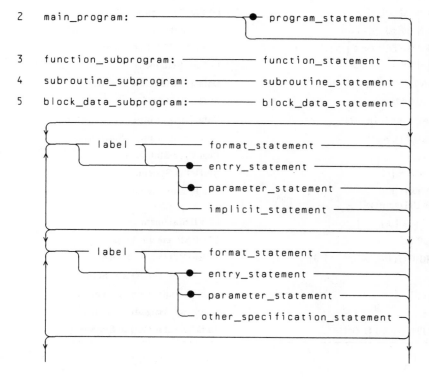

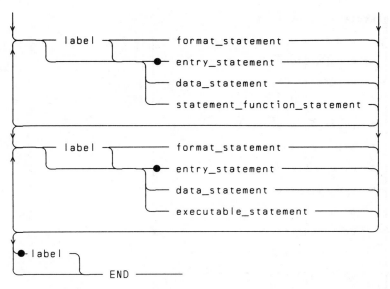

(2) A main program may not contain an ENTRY or RETURN statement.

(5) A block data subprogram may contain only BLOCK DATA, IMPLICIT, PARAMETER, DIMENSION, COMMON, SAVE, EQUIVALENCE, DATA, END, and type-statements.

6   other_specification_statement:

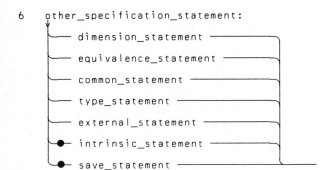

7   executable_statement:

```
    ┌─── assignment_statement ───────────┐
    ├─── goto_statement ─────────────────┤
    ├─── arithmetic_if_statement ────────┤
    ├─── logical_if_statement ───────────┤
    ●─── block_if_statement ─────────────┤
    ●─── else_if_statement ──────────────┤
    ●─── else_statement ─────────────────┤
    ●─── end_if_statement ───────────────┤
    ├─── do_statement ───────────────────┤
    ├─── continue_statement ─────────────┤
    ├─── stop_statement ─────────────────┤
    ├─── pause_statement ────────────────┤
    ├─── read_statement ─────────────────┤
    ├─── write_statement ────────────────┤
    ●─── print_statement ────────────────┤
    ├─── rewind_statement ───────────────┤
    ├─── backspace_statement ────────────┤
    ├─── endfile_statement ──────────────┤
    ●─── open_statement ─────────────────┤
    ●─── close_statement ────────────────┤
    ●─── inquire_statement ──────────────┤
    ├─── call_statement ─────────────────┤
    └─── return_statement ───────────────┘
```

(7)   An END statement is also an executable statement and
      must appear as the last statement of a program unit.

8   program_statement: ──●── PROGRAM program_name ────

9   entry_statement:

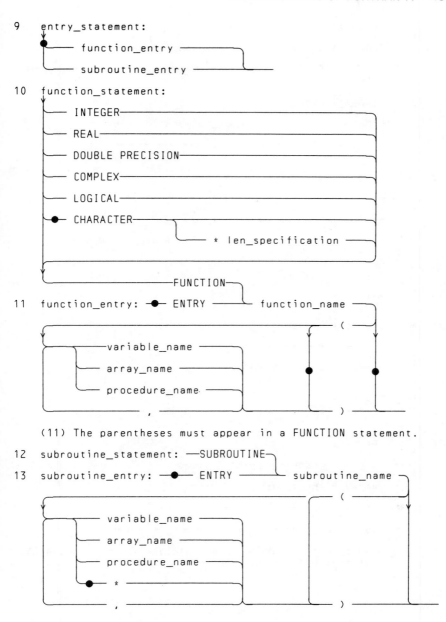

10   function_statement:

```
        INTEGER
        REAL
        DOUBLE PRECISION
        COMPLEX
        LOGICAL
        CHARACTER
                        * len_specification

                        FUNCTION
```

11   function_entry: ●— ENTRY ——— function_name

```
                            (
                variable_name
                array_name
                procedure_name
                        ,                           )
```

(11) The parentheses must appear in a FUNCTION statement.

12   subroutine_statement: —SUBROUTINE—

13   subroutine_entry: —●— ENTRY ——— subroutine_name

```
                            (
                variable_name
                array_name
                procedure_name
                ●— *
                        ,                           )
```

14   block_data_statement:

    └── BLOCK DATA ──●── block_data_subprogram_name ──

15   dimension_statement:

    └── DIMENSION ─────── array_declarator ───

16   array_declarator: ─────── array_name ───

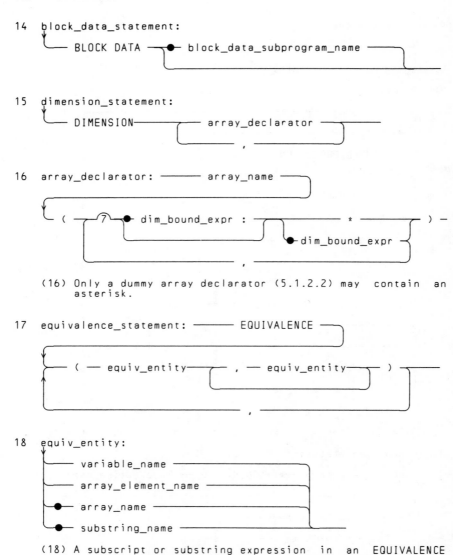

    (──7──●── dim_bound_expr : ─────── * ───) ─
                                    ●── dim_bound_expr

(16) Only a dummy array declarator (5.1.2.2) may contain an asterisk.

17   equivalence_statement: ─────── EQUIVALENCE ─

    (── equiv_entity ── , ── equiv_entity ──) ─

18   equiv_entity:

    ─── variable_name ───
    ─── array_element_name ───
    ●── array_name ───
    ●── substring_name ───

(18) A subscript or substring expression in an EQUIVALENCE statement must be an integer constant expression.

19 common_statement:

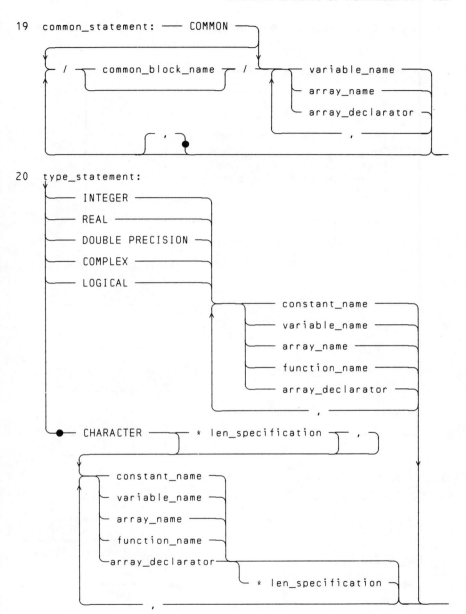

20 type_statement:

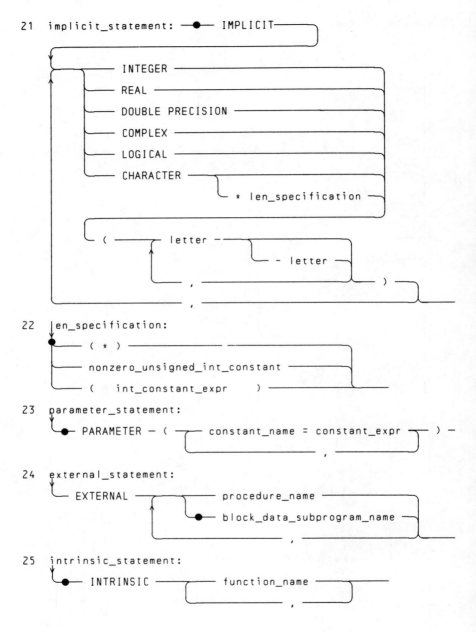

21 implicit_statement:

22 len_specification:

23 parameter_statement:

24 external_statement:

25 intrinsic_statement:

26 save_statement:

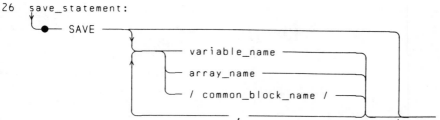

27 data_statement:

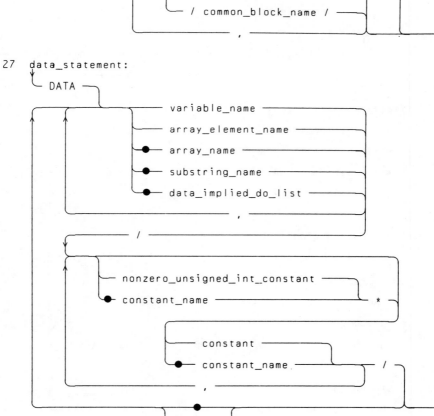

28 data_implied_do_list:

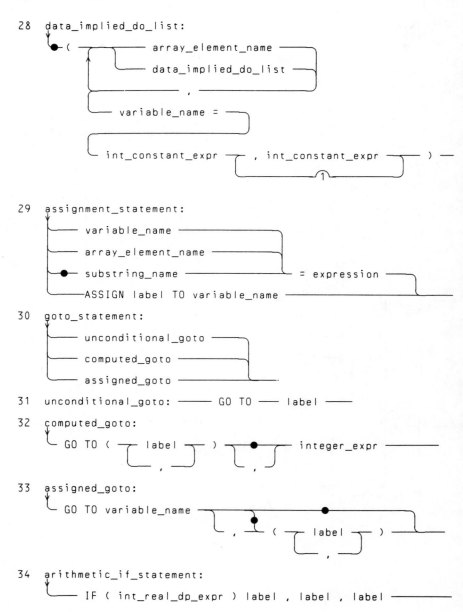

29 assignment_statement:

30 goto_statement:

31 unconditional_goto: ——— GO TO ——— label ———

32 computed_goto:

33 assigned_goto:

34 arithmetic_if_statement:

35 logical_if_statement:

    — IF (logical_expression) executable_statement ————

    (35) The executable statement contained in a logical IF
    statement must not be a DO, block IF, ELSE IF, ELSE,
    END IF, END, or another logical IF statement.

36 block_if_statement:

    — IF (logical_expression) THEN ————

37 else_if_statement:

    — ELSE IF (logical_expression) THEN ————

38 else_statement: —— ELSE ————

39 end_if_statement: —— END IF ————

40 do_statement:

    — DO label ——— , —

    —variable_name = int_real_dp_expr — , int_real_dp_expr —

41 continue_statement: ——— CONTINUE ———

42 stop_statement: —— STOP ———

43 pause_statement: —— PAUSE ———

    — digit —⟨5⟩—

    —— character_constant ——

44 write_statement: ————————— WRITE ——————————

45 read_statement: ————————— READ ——————————

46 print_statement: ——●—— PRINT ——————————

(control_info_list)

format_identifier ——— , ——— io_list

47 control_info_list:

unit_identifier

●— FMT = ——— format_identifier

●— UNIT = unit_identifier

●— REC = integer_expr

●— END = label

●— ERR = label

IOSTAT = —— variable_name

array_element_name

(47) A control_info_list must contain exactly one unit_identifier. An END= specifier must not appear in a WRITE statement.

48 io_list:

●— expression

array_name

io_implied_do_list

(48) In a READ statement, an input/output list expression must be a variable name, array element name, or substring name.

49 io_implied_do_list:

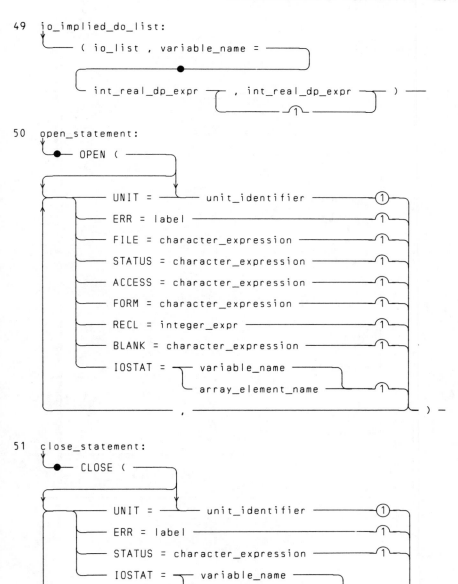

50 open_statement:

51 close_statement:

52   inquire_statement:

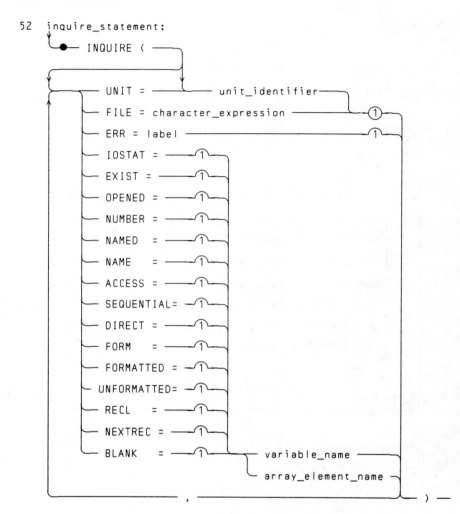

53 backspace_statement: ——— BACKSPACE

54 endfile_statement: ——— ENDFILE

55 rewind_statement: ——— REWIND

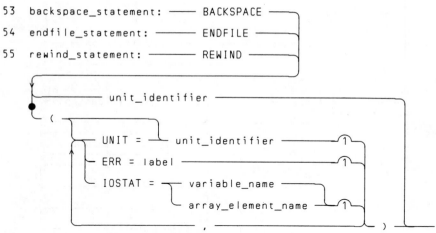

(53,54,55) BACKSPACE, ENDFILE, and REWIND statements must contain a unit identifier.

56 unit_identifier:

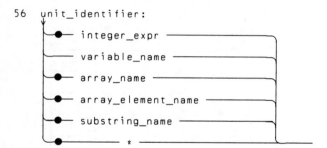

- integer_expr
- variable_name
- array_name
- array_element_name
- substring_name
- *

(56) An unit identifier must be of type integer or character, or be an asterisk.

57 format_identifier:

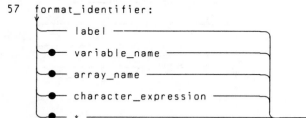

- label
- variable_name
- array_name
- character_expression
- *

(57) A format identifier that is a variable name or array name must be of type integer or character.

58 format_statement: ———— FORMAT format_specification ————

59 format_specification: — (——— fmt_specification ———) —

60 fmt_specification:

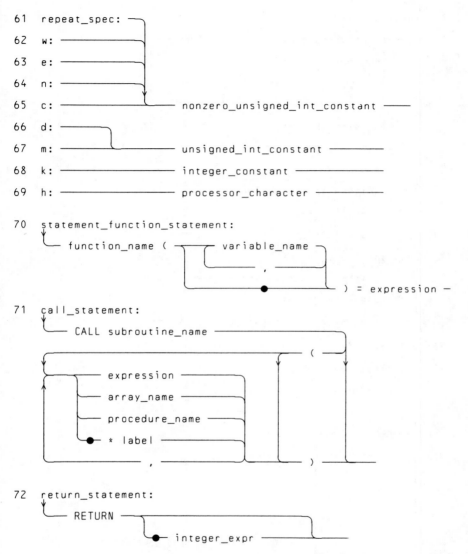

61 repeat_spec:
62 w:
63 e:
64 n:
65 c: ─────────── nonzero_unsigned_int_constant ───
66 d:
67 m: ─────────── unsigned_int_constant ─────────
68 k: ─────────── integer_constant ───────────
69 h: ─────────── processor_character ─────────

70 statement_function_statement:
        function_name (──── variable_name
                          ,
) = expression ─

71 call_statement:
        CALL subroutine_name
        (
            expression
            array_name
            procedure_name
            * label
            ,
)

72 return_statement:
        RETURN
            integer_expr

(72) An alternate return is not allowed in a function subprogram.

73 function_reference:

74 expression:

75 constant_expr:

76 arithmetic_expression:

77 integer expr:

78 int_real_dp_expr:

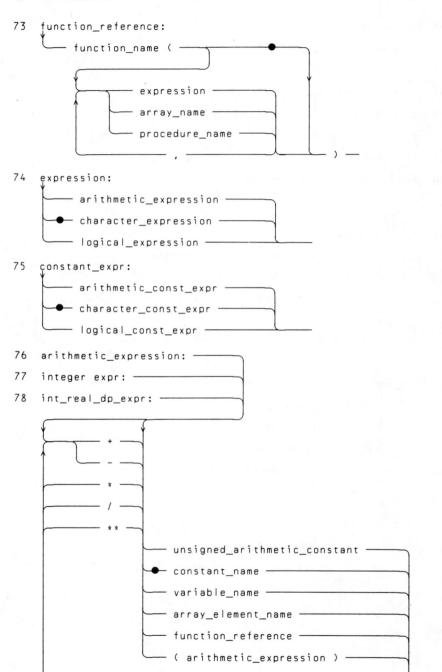

(76) A constant name, variable name, array element name, or function reference in an arithmetic expression must be of type integer, real, double precision, or complex. Tables 2 and 3 (6.1.4) list prohibited combinations involving operands of type complex.

(77) An integer expression is an arithmetic expression of type integer.

(78) An int_real_dp_expression is an arithmetic expression of type integer, real, or double precision.

79   arithmetic_const_expr:

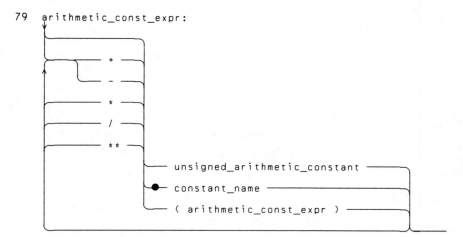

(79) A constant name in an arithmetic constant expression must be of type integer, real, double precision, or complex. Tables 2 and 3 (6.1.4) list prohibited combinations involving operands of type complex. The right hand operand (the exponent) of the ** operator must be of type integer.

80   int_constant_expr:

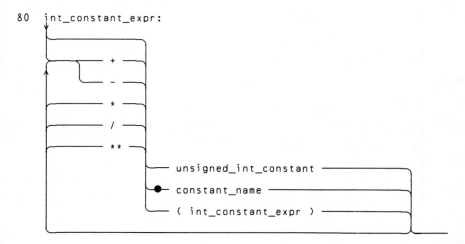

(80) A constant name in an integer constant expression must be of type integer.

81   dim_bound_expr:

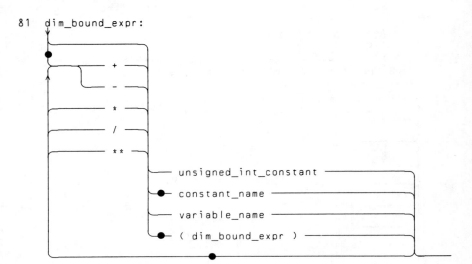

(81) Each variable name in a dimension bound expression must be of type integer and must be a dummy argument or in a common block.

82   character_expression:

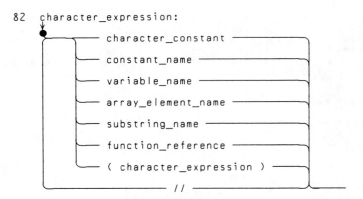

(82) A constant name, variable name, array element name, or function reference must be of type character in a character expression.

83 character_const_expr:

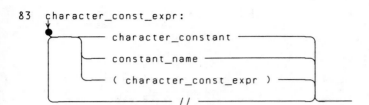

(83) A constant name must be of type character in a character
     constant expression.

84 logical_expression:

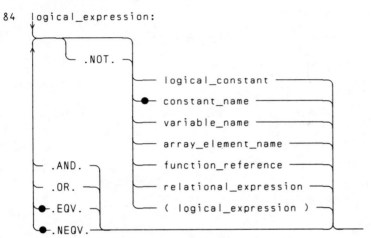

(84) A constant name, variable name, array element name, or
     function reference must be of type logical in a logical
     expression.

85 logical_const_expr:

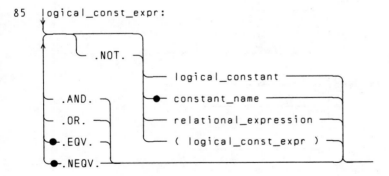

(85) A constant name must be of type logical in a logical constant expression. Also, each primary in the relational expression must be a constant expression.

86 relational_expression:

```
├─ arithmetic_expression   rel_op   arithmetic_expression ─┐
●                                                          │
└─ character_expression    rel_op   character_expression ──┘
```

(86) An arithmetic expression of type complex is permitted only when the relational operator is .EQ. or .NE.

87 rel_op:

```
┌──── .LT. ────┐
├──── .LE. ────┤
├──── .EQ. ────┤
├──── .NE. ────┤
├──── .GT. ────┤
└──── .GE. ────┘
```

88 array_element_name:

```
└── array_name ( ─●─ integer_expr ──────⟨7⟩──── ) ─
                  └──────────── , ──────────┘
```

89 substring_name:

```
●─┬── variable_name ──────┐
  └── array_element_name ─┤
  ┌──────────────────────┘
  └─ ( ─┬─ integer_expr ─┬─ : ─┬─ integer_expr ─┬─ ) ─
        └────────────────┘     └────────────────┘
```

90 constant_name: ──────────●──────────┐
91 variable_name: ──────────────────────┤
92 array_name: ────────────────────────┤
93 common_block_name: ──────────────────┤
94 program_name: ───────────●───────────┤
95 block_data_subprogram_name: ───●──────┘

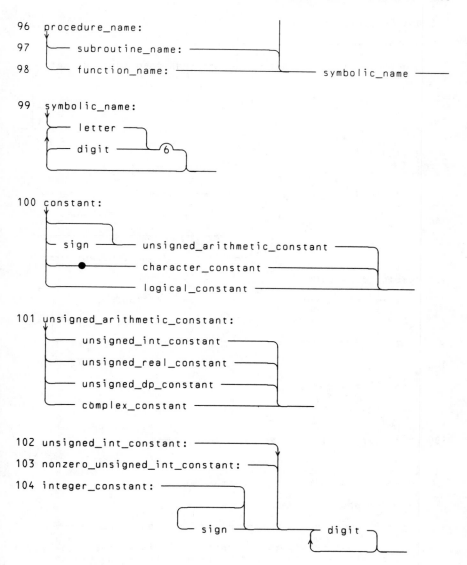

96 procedure_name:

97 ├── subroutine_name: ─────────

98 └── function_name: ───────────── symbolic_name ───

99 symbolic_name:

├── letter ───
├── digit ─── 6

100 constant:

├── sign ──── unsigned_arithmetic_constant ───
├── ● ──── character_constant ───
└── ──── logical_constant ───

101 unsigned_arithmetic_constant:

├── unsigned_int_constant ───
├── unsigned_real_constant ───
├── unsigned_dp_constant ───
└── complex_constant ───

102 unsigned_int_constant: ─────────

103 nonzero_unsigned_int_constant: ───

104 integer_constant: ─────────

└── sign ───┘   ┌── digit ───┐

(103) A nonzero, unsigned, integer constant must contain a
nonzero digit.

105 unsigned_real_constant:

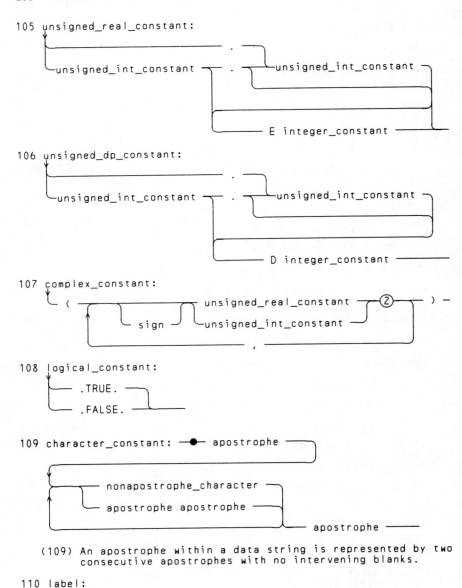

106 unsigned_dp_constant:

107 complex_constant:

108 logical_constant:

109 character_constant:

(109) An apostrophe within a data string is represented by two consecutive apostrophes with no intervening blanks.

110 label:

(110) A label must contain a nonzero digit.

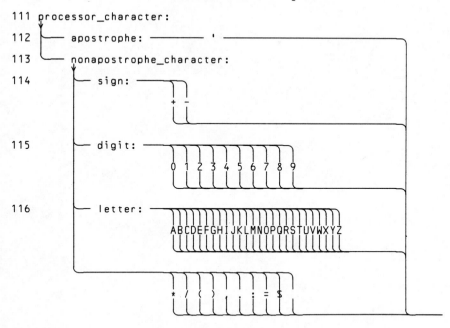

(111) A blank is a processor character. The set of processor
      characters may include additional characters recognized
      by the processor.

INDEX†

†An asterisk (*) following a page reference denotes a syntax chart specification.